IN MY NAME

Understanding the Believer's Authority Over the Powers of Darkness

By Kirk A. DuBois

Unless otherwise indicated, Scripture quotations are taken from the King James Version of the Bible.

Scripture quotations marked NKJV are taken from the New King James Version.® Copyright © 1982 by Thomas Nelson. Used by permission. All rights reserved.

Scripture quotations marked AMPC are taken from the Amplified Bible Classic, Copyright © 1954, 1958, 1962, 1964, 1965, 1987 by The Lockman Foundation. Used by permission.

Scripture quotations marked NIV are taken from the Holy Bible, New International Version®, NIV®. Copyright © 1973, 1978, 1984, 2011 by Biblica, Inc.™ Used by permission of Zondervan. All rights reserved worldwide. www.zondervan.com The "NIV" and "New International Version" are trademarks registered in the United States Patent and Trademark Office by Biblica, Inc.™

Scripture quotations marked ONMB are taken from One New Man Bible. Copyright © 2011 by True Potential Publishing.

Copyright © 2019
by Kirk A. DuBois
Broken Arrow, OK

First printing: May 2019
Second printing: August 2019
Third printing: February 2020
Fourth printing: March 2021

Published by Harvest International Ministries
PO Box 1309
Broken Arrow, OK 74013
All rights reserved.
Printed in the United States of America.

ISBN 978-1-733-98480-5

Library of Congress Control Number: 2019904702

ENDORSEMENTS

As a spoken and demonstrated authority, Dr. Kirk DuBois draws from his powerful Christian walk and Biblical research of over 48 years to present Christian believers this masterpiece, *In My Name*. For too long, many have failed to accept the complete and FINISHED work of Jesus Christ. Folks adopt a Jesus Plus Additives mentality. Dr. Kirk, in a mandate from the Holy Spirit has delivered this great manuscript to help believers stake our rightful claim to spiritual authority by the Power of faith in God's Word. Learn how to walk in freedom and God's liberties to us. Witness a fleeing devil. Fulfill your destiny with joy and win others to Jesus Christ.

In My Name is an essential and indispensable wellspring of your personal library, or as part of any Bible school curriculum.

— *Dr. Stephen Anderson,*
President,
Transworld Accrediting Commission International

Dr. Kirk DuBois' *In My Name*, is one of the first books that guides believers through the heights and depths of understanding Christ-centered authority. Balancing positional, reconstructive and scriptural authority, DuBois gives believers a rightful place in the battle against "principalities, powers, and the rulers of the darkness" (Eph. 6:12, NKJV). If Frank Peretti's series represents prose on spiritual warfare, *In My Name*, gives believers the roadmap on how to overcome in spiritual warfare.

— *Steven Long,*
Director of Regional Ministry Development and Executive Pastor
Grand Canyon University

In his book, *In My Name*, Dr. Kirk DuBois takes a fresh look at the scriptural truths concerning the Body of Christ's authority over Satan. Chapter by chapter he builds a solid Biblical case for the reader and then challenges the believer to take his rightful position in prayer. Get your Bible and notebook ready as Dr. DuBois takes you on the Scriptural journey into the authority we have in Christ. *In My Name* is a must read and it is my honor to recommend it.

— Dr. Tad Gregurich, D. Min.
President, Gregurich Ministries
Reaching People to Reach the World

At the turn of the 20th Century, the body of Christ was delivered a much fought for revelation on the authority of the believer from China Inland Mission director John A. MacMillan's private prayer journals.

Built upon a great heritage Dr. DuBois takes us on a deeper journey into divine authority for this century of believers. Dr. DuBois brings this truth to the next generation.

I am convinced this book should be taught in every seminary worldwide whether Charismatic or Fundamental, as these truths cross denominational lines.

— Joseph R. Castillo, D. D.,
Bishop of All Nations International Fellowship,
S. E. Asia

TABLE OF CONTENTS

Foreword 7

SECTION 1: The Scriptural Foundation for the Believer's Authority

1. The Power of Knowing You Are Already Free 13

2. The Foundation of Our Authority 19

3. The Church from God's Perspective 33

4. Authority Given—Authority Lost 67

5. Son of Adam—Son of God 89

SECTION 2: The Scriptural Restoration of the Believer's Authority

6. Crucifixion, Death, Burial, Resurrection and Ascension 117

7. Authority Regained 145

8. The Name and What It Means 163

9. The Present-Day Ministry of Jesus 183

SECTION 3: Practical Application: How to Use His Authority

10. How Do I Use Authority? 193

11. Submission and Authority 211

12. Authority in Prayer 223

13. Overcoming Scriptures 251

FOREWORD

For more than forty years, I have been fascinated with the subject of the believer's authority. This desire has led me to search the Word of God for answers to many questions I've had about this very important subject. Of course, when we hunger for knowledge and revelation, the Holy Spirit becomes our Teacher, and the floodgates of Heaven begin to open. I want to share with you the revelation the Lord has brought to me and help you discover who you are in Christ as well as the authority we have as members of His Body.

There are three important points I want to make clear as you read this book so that you properly understand this teaching on spiritual authority.

First, when I refer to the "Church," I am not speaking of any denomination, Catholic or Orthodox body, organization or corporation of man. Nor am I speaking of any earthly city or headquarters of any group. I am talking about what the New Testament calls the "Church"—a Body of Believers in Jesus Christ, the risen Son of God, who have been born again and follow Him through the power of the Holy Spirit. The Bible calls this group the "Church," "Body of Christ," "the Temple of the Holy Spirit," and other titles. This true Church is made up of all kinds of people who may or may not belong to various organizations, denominations, and so on, but they are members of the true, invisible Church, which is His Body.

The New Testament Greek word for "Church" is Ekklesia, which means "called out (people), a congregation, a meeting" and is similar to one of the Old Testament words in Hebrew meaning "congregation" or "assembly."

The second important point I want to make clear from the beginning as I build a case for the importance of the Church in God's plan is that in no way do I subscribe to the doctrine of what is known as "replacement theology." I do not believe the Church replaced Israel. God still has promises and a purpose for the natural seed of Abraham that have yet to be completed. The ultimate completion of all that has been promised to them will be realized when they come to recognize Yeshua as the Mashiach (Jesus as the Messiah).

> **Zechariah 12:10**
>
> *And I will pour upon the house of David, and upon the inhabitants of Jerusalem, the spirit of grace and of supplications: and they shall look upon me whom they have pierced, and they shall mourn for him, as one mourneth for his only son, and shall be in bitterness for him, as one that is in bitterness for his firstborn.*

Having said that, I believe the Church is to be the "one new man" Paul talks about in Ephesians, where both Jew and Gentile become one.

Finally, the third important point you need to understand is that when I refer to the believer's spiritual authority, reigning in life, overcoming, the Kingdom of God, and ruling with Christ, I am not talking about ruling over people's free will, taking over the Earth, natural warfare, and similar activities.

Jesus told Pilate, *My Kingdom is not of this world: if My Kingdom were of this world, then would My servants fight, that I should not be delivered to the Jews: but now is My Kingdom not from hence* (John 18:36). He also said, *Neither shall they say, Lo here! or, lo there! for, be-*

hold, the Kingdom of God is within you (Luke 17:21), and, *But if I cast out devils by the Spirit of God, then the Kingdom of God is come unto you* (Matthew 12:28). St. Paul said, *For the Kingdom of God is not meat and drink; but righteousness, and peace, and joy in the Holy Ghost* (Romans 14:17), and, *For the Kingdom of God is not in word, but in power* (1 Corinthians 4:20).

We are talking about a spiritual Kingdom (which will one day become an earthly kingdom on the Earth after Jesus returns) with spiritual authority over spirits, and over your life and ministry. The real estate of this Kingdom is people. Every time a person gives their life to Jesus, the Kingdom of God expands. Every time a person is set free from the demonic forces of evil, the Kingdom of God advances.

This *…whole world lieth in wickedness* (1 John 5:19) under the influence of *the prince of the power of the air, the spirit that now worketh in the children of disobedience* (Ephesians 2:2), also called *the god of this world (that) hath blinded the minds of them which believe not* (2 Corinthians 4:4). Our battle is *not against flesh and blood, but against principalities, against powers, against the rulers of the darkness of this world, against spiritual wickedness in high places* (Ephesians 6:12).

But believers in Christ are not under the rules of the devil's kingdom because Jesus *hath delivered us from the power of darkness, and hath translated us into the Kingdom of His dear Son: in whom we have redemption through His blood, even the forgiveness of sins* (Colossians 1:13–14). We are to learn to use our authority to lead a victorious life: *much more they which receive abundance of grace and of the gift of righteousness shall reign in life by one, Jesus Christ* (Romans 5:17). *Ye are of God, little children, and have overcome them: because greater is He that is in you, than he that is in the world* (1 John 4:4).

God desires us to learn to overcome in life. This life is a "boot camp" to learn to overcome now, so we can reign with Him in the next age. This life is "training for reigning."

The goal of this book is to fire up a generation of powerful prayer warriors who know their rights and authority in Jesus Christ and take their place as co-laborers with Him in prayer. I give this warning to you if you are serious about learning these truths: the devil does not want you to know these things, and he will try anything he can to stop you, discourage you, and distract you. You will become a threat to his plans when you know who you are in Christ, and what you have in Him.

Are you ready to advance? Then keep reading…

SECTION 1:

The Scriptural Foundation for the Believer's Authority

CHAPTER 1

THE POWER OF KNOWING YOU ARE ALREADY FREE

What would you do if someone came up behind you, poked his finger in your back, and said, "I have a gun. Give me your money"? Most people would instantly become fearful and comply with whatever was demanded of them—because they believe the robber has a gun. Their fear would be real, *but the threat would not*. As long as the truth was kept from them, they would be bound by the thief's deception and forced to comply with his demands, even though the thief has no actual weapon to enforce his will.

The same could be said of the Emancipation Proclamation made by President Lincoln during the U.S. Civil War. Any slaves who did not hear of the proclamation would have continued to believe they were slaves to their master—*even though they had already been set free*.

Over the centuries, a lack of knowledge of the truth has harmed people in every nation, in many situations. And this form of deception is exactly what the devil has done to the Church. He has deceived us into submitting to him, even though he has been effectively disarmed through the work of Jesus Christ on the Cross. For believers, the Bible is our emancipation proclamation. We have been set free.

Unfortunately, though, most Christians don't realize it. They don't know they are already free. They don't know what they are entitled to, by right, as citizens of God's Kingdom. They don't know they already rule and reign over the devil. As a result, they continue to be bound by the devil, even though Jesus has set them free through His death, burial, and resurrection.

This misconception, this lack of understanding, leads to much suffering in the lives of Christians—suffering we would not have to endure if we understood that Jesus already won our freedom and has paved for us a better way than what the devil has to offer. So, it is absolutely crucial that we know what we are entitled to, through Christ.

We Are Citizens of a Heavenly Kingdom

In order for us to understand our freedom and the authority we have in Christ, we must first understand how kingdoms function—and which kingdom we belong to as believers in Christ.

Simply put, the Bible is a book about kingdoms. In fact, it's also the handbook of your citizenship in God's Kingdom. Colossians 1:13 says that God has delivered us from the power (the control and dominion) of darkness and has translated us into (made us citizens of) the Kingdom of His dear Son. This verse establishes the fact that there are two kingdoms in existence, and that we no longer belong to, or are under the authority of, the kingdom of darkness. We are now citizens of another kingdom—the Kingdom of God—the Kingdom of His dear Son, Jesus!

Jesus preached that the Kingdom of God was at hand, meaning that the Kingdom of God had arrived. Jesus was the new King in town, and He was playing by new rules! What does that look like in practice? Let's take a look at what the Bible says.

Jesus announced, *The Spirit of the Lord is upon Me, because He hath anointed Me to preach the gospel to the poor; He hath sent Me to heal the brokenhearted, to preach deliverance to the captives, and recovering of sight to the blind, to set at liberty them that are bruised, to preach the acceptable year of the Lord* (Luke 4:18–19). Jesus was anointed to announce the arrival of God's Kingdom, *and* He was anointed King of the newly arrived Kingdom!

In Acts 10:38 the Apostle Peter said, *How God anointed Jesus of Nazareth with the Holy Ghost and with power: who went about doing good, and healing all that were oppressed of the devil; for God was with Him.* As King of the newly arrived Kingdom, Jesus exercised authority over the kingdom of darkness and displaced it wherever He went.

We can also tell from these two verses how the two kingdoms differ. The kingdom of darkness—ruled by Satan as a result of Adam's sin (which we'll discuss in more detail in chapter 4)—is characterized by poverty, broken-heartedness, slavery, captivity, blindness, bruising, sickness, wrongdoing…and every manner of suffering, loss, lack, and wickedness that you can imagine.

But Jesus didn't come to tell us to keep suffering, did He? He came instead to bring us into His Kingdom—a Kingdom characterized by truth, abundance, freedom, joy, vision, wellness, wholeness, healing, doing right…and every manner of fullness and goodness you can imagine.

Which kingdom would you prefer to live in? It's an easy decision, isn't it? You'd want to live in God's Kingdom. And as a believer in Christ, you *do* live there. You have become a citizen of Heaven.

Your Citizenship Is Here and Now

Many people have assumed that their citizenship begins when they reach Heaven, not on Earth. But Jesus also showed us where and when the Kingdom was to be established. Jesus said, *Behold, the Kingdom of God is within you* (Luke 17:21). The real estate of the new Kingdom is the hearts of men. It is something that exists here and now, within every believer.

As we explore each facet of Kingdom authority and our part in it, we will recognize that everything Jesus has given to us is based upon His death, burial and resurrection. It was through His death and resurrection that He destroyed the devil's power and was given the Name above every name. Through His ascension to Heaven, He is seated at God's right hand, far above the devil, ruling over him.

If you are a Christian, that means you are in Christ; you belong to Him as a part of His Body (1 Corinthians 12:27; Ephesians 4:15–16). You are seated with Him in heavenly places (Ephesians 2:6). Everything that is under His feet is also under your feet (Ephesians 1:22). No Christian should ever be afraid of demons or the devil, because they are all under our feet. In Hebrews 2:14–15, the Word of God says that Jesus destroyed the devil and delivered us from the devil's bondage of fear. We do not need to fear him anymore, because he has been defeated.

As you will come to see as you read this book, the only way Satan can operate in this Earth is to find people who will give him place in their lives and allow him to use them for his purposes. Since there are unbelievers and wicked people on the Earth, he can work through them. However, he doesn't own believers anymore because we have been purchased by the blood of Jesus Christ!

THE POWER OF KNOWING YOU ARE ALREADY FREE

So, why do so many Christians live as though the devil rules over them?

In 2 Corinthians 4:4, we read that Satan, the god of this world, has blinded the eyes of the unbelievers. People who are ignorant and blind cannot see the truth. This applies to Christians as well. The Bible says in Hosea 4:6, *My people are destroyed for lack of knowledge.* Through ignorance, or being blind to the truth, God's people get into trouble. But Paul said to the Ephesian Christians, "I pray that your eyes would be opened, so that you would see the great power that God has toward you" (Ephesians 1:18–19).

What does this revelation do for us? Here's one example from recent Christian history.

A man named Smith Wigglesworth from England in the early 1900s established a worldwide healing ministry before his death in 1947. He raised over twenty people from the dead and cast out many demons. I heard an older British minister, who knew Wigglesworth and has since gone to Heaven, tell of one time how, while Wigglesworth was on the mission field overseas, the devil appeared to him in the middle of the night. The wind had blown the window shutters open, and Wigglesworth awoke to see the devil in his room.

When he saw him, Wigglesworth said, "Oh, it's you." And then he simply turned over and went back to sleep. He wasn't scared or moved by the devil's appearance in his room, because he knew who he was in Christ.[1]

Wigglesworth knew he had authority over the devil. And so do you!

In John 8:31–32 (NKJV), Jesus told His followers, *If you abide in My Word, you are My disciples indeed. And you shall know the truth,*

[1] Hibbert, A. (2009). Smith Wigglesworth: The secret of his power. Tulsa, OK: Harrison House.

and the truth shall make you free. Truth always liberates us. Within the pages of this book, you will discover the truth about who you are in Christ, and what you have in Him, so you will never again be afraid of the devil. Instead, you will learn to exercise authority over the devil, just like Jesus did.

CHAPTER 2

THE FOUNDATION OF OUR AUTHORITY

That at the Name of Jesus every knee should bow, of things in Heaven, and things in Earth, and things under the Earth.

—Philippians 2:10

This Scripture tells us that the authority of Jesus Christ is recognized in three worlds: in Heaven, in the Earth, and under the Earth. The question is, do *we* recognize His authority? All of Heaven knows the authority that is in the Name of Jesus. All of hell knows the authority that is in the Name of Jesus. Even creation itself, the Earth, knows the authority in the Name of Jesus.

But do *we* recognize it?

If only we knew what the devil already knows about us, we wouldn't be afraid of him anymore. He knows who we really are. He knows what is really inside of us. The Bible says even the demons believe in Jesus, and they shudder in fear (James 2:19). The Bible says if we resist the devil, he will flee from us in terror (James 4:7). The devil knows more about our authority over him than most of us know!

But take heart, because Jesus said if we continue in His Word, we will know the truth and the truth will make us free (John 8:31–32). Continue reading the Bible, and you will find out the truth about who you are in Christ, what you have in Him, and what the devil no longer has authority to do in your life. Continue reading this book too, because I am going to pull the covers off the lies of the devil, and reveal through the Scriptures how he is under our feet.

Our Position in Christ

Ephesians 1:15—2:9

Wherefore I also, after I heard of your faith in the Lord Jesus, and love unto all the saints,

Cease not to give thanks for you, making mention of you in my prayers;

That the God of our Lord Jesus Christ, the Father of glory, may give unto you the spirit of wisdom and revelation in the knowledge of Him:

The eyes of your understanding being enlightened; that ye may know what is the hope of His calling, and what the riches of the glory of His inheritance in the saints,

And what is the exceeding greatness of His power to us-ward who believe, according to the working of His mighty power,

Which He wrought in Christ, when He raised Him from the dead, and set Him at His own right hand in the heavenly places,

Far above all principality, and power, and might, and dominion, and every name that is named, not only in this world, but also in that which is to come:

And hath put all things under His feet, and gave Him to be the head over all things to the Church,

Which is His Body, the fulness of Him that filleth all in all.

And you hath He quickened, who were dead in trespasses and sins;

Wherein in time past ye walked according to the course of this world, according to the prince of the power of the air, the spirit that now worketh in the children of disobedience:

Among whom also we all had our conversation in times past in the lusts of our flesh, fulfilling the desires of the flesh and of the mind; and were by nature the children of wrath, even as others.

But God, who is rich in mercy, for His great love wherewith He loved us,

Even when we were dead in sins, hath quickened us together with Christ, (by grace ye are saved;)

And hath raised us up together, and made us sit together in heavenly places in Christ Jesus:

That in the ages to come He might shew the exceeding riches of His grace in His kindness toward us through Christ Jesus.

For by grace are ye saved through faith; and that not of yourselves: it is the gift of God:

Not of works, lest any man should boast.

This passage of Scripture is the chief foundation for what we need to know about our authority in Jesus Christ. The Apostle Paul prayed that the eyes of the Ephesian Christians would be opened, so that they would understand the great power that God displays on our behalf—the very same power that is at work within us, and that we can tap into, by faith.

It's essential to understand how powerful we are in Him. So I encourage you to pray this prayer over yourself right now:

> *"God, open my eyes. Give me a spirit of wisdom and revelation to know the exceeding greatness of Your power. Teach me and reveal Your truth to me, so I will know the hope of Your calling and the riches of Your glory. Amen!"*

Now, believe that the Holy Spirit is opening your eyes.

Paul prayed a similar prayer because he wanted the Christians of his day to know the exceeding greatness of God's power. This was the same power that worked in Christ when God raised Him from the dead. When He raised Him from the dead, He seated Him in heavenly places far above all principalities and powers. He put everything under His feet and made Jesus the head of the Church, which is His body.

Paul said that this power was "great" toward those who believe. The *Amplified Classic* version (AMPC) says His power is *immeasurable*, *unlimited*, and *surpassingly great*—and it's working in and for us! If you are a believer, then the same resurrection power that raised Jesus from the dead is unlimited, immeasurable, and surpassingly great toward you. If Jesus is seated in heavenly places with all principalities and powers—that is, all the power of the devil—under His feet, then we, as His body, are seated there too!

As long as you are in the Body of Christ, it doesn't matter where you are; the devil is under your feet. Physically, you may be sitting in your easy chair right now, but in the spiritual realm, you are seated with Christ. This authority and this victory that we have are not going to happen sometime in the future after you die and go to heaven. No, *right now* you are seated with Christ in heavenly places. The devil already knows that, but now you do too!

The Three Things All Christians Need to Know

I want to help you understand the authority of the believer because I know it will change your life when you learn what God has already done for you. I am going to lay a foundation of biblical truth and then build on it throughout this book. A foundation is vital to any building, especially if the builders expect the structure to stand the test of time. I want you to have a strong foundation that will stand the test of time and the assaults of the enemy, so that you will continue to walk in victory throughout your whole life, from this day forward.

Let's begin building the foundation by looking again at Ephesians chapter 1 as the Apostle Paul writes to the believers in Ephesus about his prayers for them.

Ephesians chapter 1 reveals that Paul wanted Christians to understand three things. The first point he wanted us to grasp is found in verse 18: to know the hope of our calling. The second truth he wanted for us is that we would know the riches of God's glory and His inheritance in us, the saints. The third point is in verse 19. Paul said that he wanted us to know the exceeding greatness of God's power toward those who believe in Him.

The Apostle Paul explains this power this way: He says it is according to the working of God's mighty power, which He worked in Christ when He raised Him from the dead and set Him at His right hand in heavenly places. This resurrecting power was so great that it caused Jesus, Who had paid the eternal price for our sins, to be raised from the dead and to be seated at the right hand of the Father. In verse 21, we see that His position is far above all principality and power, every might and place of authority, and every name that can be used or assigned, not only in this world, but also in the world to come. God has

IN MY NAME

put all things under Jesus' feet and made Him the head of the Church.

Paul says the power that God displays toward us, on our behalf and in us who believe Him, is the same power that brought about the resurrection, victory, and exaltation of Jesus Christ over all the power of the devil (Eph. 1:20-21). God also exerted this power when He made Jesus to be head of the Church, which is His body (Eph. 1:22).

Remember, the Church is the Body of Christ in the Earth. As part of His Body, we are intricately connected to Him and all that He has. We share in His power and authority.

When God raised Jesus from the dead, He put every demon and fallen angel under His feet. I want you to take a look at your feet right now. Where are they located? Are they just under your head, or are they under your entire body? Your feet are located in the very last position, under the rest of your body.

Jesus is the head of the Body. But He calls us, the Church, His Body. This passage says that God put everything under Jesus' feet. And if God put everything under Jesus' feet, then where does that leave us? If we are His Body, and if God has put all things under Jesus' feet, then He's put everything under our feet too! We are positioned above the devil in authority, not beneath him. It doesn't matter if you've been a Christian for fifty years or a single day. If you are a part of the Body of Christ, then all things are under your feet also.

Before we continue, it is important to realize that when Ephesians was written, it was a letter from Paul to the believers in Ephesus, and it did not contain chapters or verses. You probably don't write letters with chapters and verses, and neither did Paul. The chapters and verses were added later to help us find things easier. An added chapter break doesn't mean that a thought has stopped or changed. As Ephesians chapter 1 transitions into chapter 2, it is a continuation of the same prayer, the prayer that we might have our spiritual eyes opened and know the greatness of God's power toward believers. We must understand that the same power that raised Christ from the dead also placed Him—and us as His body—over all principalities and powers, whether angelic or demonic.

How do we know this? Ephesians 6:12 says, *We wrestle not against flesh and blood, but against principalities, against powers, against the rulers of the darkness of this world, against spiritual wickedness in high places.* These principalities, the same ones mentioned in Ephesians chapter 1, are demonic spirits that were put under Jesus' feet when He rose from the dead. And that's where they still are—under His feet, and ours.

As we read Ephesians chapter 2, Paul says that though we used to be dead in sins, God made us alive in Christ. In verse 2, he continues to say that we all used to be under the control of the disobedient spirit, Satan. Verses 4 through 6 tell us that because of His love and mercy, God raised us up to sit with Christ in heavenly places even while we were dead in sin. This is what Paul is praying that we Christians would see—God's great power toward us—His power to deliver us, forgive us, and raise us up to a place of authority in Christ, not because we earned it, but because of His own power to forgive us and save us through His own grace. When He raised Jesus up and set Him at His right hand, putting the devil under His feet, we were raised up with Him in heavenly places, with everything under our feet too. Sometimes it doesn't always look like everything is under our feet, but it always is.

The Name Above All Names

Let's look at another foundational Scripture for understanding who we are in Christ and the authority we have in Him.

Philippians 2:5–11

Let this mind be in you, which was also in Christ Jesus:

Who, being in the form of God, thought it not robbery to be equal with God:

But made Himself of no reputation, and took upon Him the form of a servant, and was made in the likeness of men:

And being found in fashion as a man, He humbled Himself, and became obedient unto death, even the death of the Cross.

Wherefore God also hath highly exalted Him, and given Him a Name which is above every name:

That at the Name of Jesus every knee should bow, of things in heaven, and things in Earth, and things under the Earth;

And that every tongue should confess that Jesus Christ is Lord, to the glory of God the Father.

Notice in this passage that God the Father has exalted Jesus and given Him a Name above every other name in Heaven, in the Earth, and under the Earth. Every knee will bow and every tongue will confess, in all three realms, that Jesus Christ is Lord.

Hebrews 1:2–5

[God] hath in these last days spoken unto us by His Son, whom He hath appointed heir of all things, by whom also He made the worlds;

Who being the brightness of His glory, and the express image of His person, and upholding all things by the word of His power, when He had by Himself purged our sins, sat down on the right hand of the Majesty on high:

Being made so much better than the angels, as He hath by inheritance obtained a more excellent Name than they.

For unto which of the angels said He at any time, Thou art My Son, this day have I begotten Thee? And again, I will be to Him a Father, and He shall be to Me a Son?

These verses tell us that God is now speaking to us through His Son, Jesus Christ. He made Him the heir of the world. According to Hebrews 1:4, Jesus was made better than the angels, and by inheritance Jesus acquired a Name better than they have. Here again, the Bible reveals the greatness of the Name of Jesus. According to Ephesians and Philippians, this greatness was bestowed upon His Name at the resurrection. It is restated in Hebrews 1:4 when it says He obtained a better name by inheritance. And verse 5 shows us when that happened.

Let's consider Hebrews 1:5, which says, *For unto which of the angels said He at any time, "Thou art My Son, this day have I begotten Thee?" And again, "I will be to Him a Father, and He shall be to Me a Son?"*

When did God say, "You are My Son. Today have I begotten You"? There were actually three times when God said something like this to Jesus. The first time was during His baptism by John in the Jordan River, when He said, *"This is My beloved Son, in whom I am well pleased"* (Matthew 3:17).

The second time occurred when Peter, James, and John went up onto a mountaintop with Jesus (Matthew 17:1-8). A bright cloud came down and overshadowed them. Jesus was changed into the brightness of God's glory. Then Peter said, "Let's build three tabernacles—one for You, one for Moses, and one for Elijah." Suddenly, a voice came out of the cloud, saying, "This is My beloved Son; listen to Him."

The third time occurs in Hebrew 1:5 when God the Father says, "You are My beloved Son; this day have I begotten You"—that is, given You birth. The writer is actually quoting from a prophecy about Jesus Christ found in the Psalms.

> **Psalm 2:6–12**
>
> *Yet have I set my king upon my holy hill of Zion.*
>
> *I will declare the decree: the Lord hath said unto me, Thou art my Son; this day have I begotten thee.*
>
> *Ask of me, and I shall give thee the heathen for thine inheritance, and the uttermost parts of the Earth for thy possession.*
>
> *Thou shalt break them with a rod of iron; thou shalt dash them in pieces like a potter's vessel.*
>
> *Be wise now therefore, O ye kings: be instructed, ye judges of the Earth.*
>
> *Serve the Lord with fear, and rejoice with trembling.*
>
> *Kiss the Son, lest he be angry, and ye perish from the way, when his wrath is kindled but a little. Blessed are all they that put their trust in him.*

When does the Father say, "You are My beloved Son; this day have I begotten You"? Verse 6 of this passage reveals the answer. He says it after He has set Jesus as the King upon the holy hill of Zion and given Him the Name above all names. This can only be *after the resurrection*.

When Paul was preaching in Acts, he again restates the prophecy from Psalm 2 and directly connects this declaration with the resurrection of Jesus.

Acts 13:32–34

And we declare unto you glad tidings, how that the promise which was made unto the fathers,

God hath fulfilled the same unto us their children, in that He hath raised up Jesus again; as it is also written in the second psalm, Thou art My Son, this day have I begotten Thee.

And as concerning that He raised Him up from the dead, now no more to return to corruption, He said on this wise, I will give You the sure mercies of David.

From these passages of Scripture, it is clear that phrase, "Thou art My Son; this day have I begotten Thee," refers to Jesus having been raised from the dead and exalted over the devil and over every evil thing. He has been exalted already over sin, sickness, poverty, and all other forms of evil and destruction. And because we are in Him, and a part of His Body, we share in the authority He has been given by God the Father.

The Truth Has Been Revealed

The truth of our authority has been revealed through the Scriptures. The key is, and always will be, do we realize it? And do we know how to act on it? This is why Paul, in Ephesians 1:17, prays for the Christians of his day to have revelation. And we should pray the same prayer over ourselves today, as we continue to learn and grow as believers.

When we pray for a spirit of revelation, we are asking that things would be revealed to us. In this verse, the Greek word for *revelation* means "to be exposed," as if someone has removed his or her clothing. If something is hidden, it is not exposed or revealed. God wants to reveal or expose the truth to us about who we are in Christ and what we have in Him.

2 Corinthians 4:4–7

In whom the god of this world hath blinded the minds of them which believe not, lest the light of the glorious gospel of Christ, who is the image of God, should shine unto them.

For we preach not ourselves, but Christ Jesus the Lord; and ourselves your servants for Jesus' sake.

For God, who commanded the light to shine out of darkness, hath shined in our hearts, to give the light of the knowledge of the glory of God in the face of Jesus Christ.

But we have this treasure in earthen vessels, that the excellency of the power may be of God, and not of us.

This passage reveals that the god of this world, Satan, wants to blind the minds of people from seeing the light of the knowledge of the glory of God—the light of the glorious gospel of Christ. But God wants us to see it. He desires for the light of the knowledge that Christ has set us free to shine in our hearts. This treasure is hidden inside of us, as earthen vessels, and God wants the light to shine out from us so that others can see it and be free as well.

Do you want this for yourself? Do you want to see what God wants you to see? According to the Word of God, it is His will for every believer to know who they are in Christ and to walk in all the fullness of

God. Do you realize that it is God's will for you, as a believer, to have a spirit of wisdom and revelation in the knowledge of Jesus Christ?

The Bible says that if we pray according to His will, then we will have what we ask for (1 John 5:14-15). As a believer, you have the right to ask for understanding. So pray this prayer and believe in your heart that God hears you when you pray:

> *Father God, I pray that You give me a spirit of wisdom and revelation in the knowledge of Jesus Christ. I pray that my eyes would be open, that I might know the hope of my calling, and the riches of Your glory in the saints. And I pray that I might know the exceeding greatness of Your power that You have toward me because I believe in Christ. In Jesus' Name. Amen.*

As we explore these truths throughout this book, remember to pray this prayer for yourself daily. Allow God to bring fresh revelation into your heart about His power and glory at work in you, and the truth of who you are in Him. Allow God to open your eyes to the wonderful truths of His Word.

CHAPTER 3

THE CHURCH FROM GOD'S PERSPECTIVE

Human beings often label each other and categorize each other by a multitude of traits—how we look, where we were born, where we live, how many possessions we own, and just about any other trait you can imagine. But God does not see us through these lenses and labels. Instead, God recognizes only three groups of people in the Earth. The Apostle Paul acknowledges these groups in 1 Corinthians 10:32, which says, *Give none offence, neither to the Jews, nor to the Gentiles, nor to the Church of God.* From God's perspective, every person on Earth is a member of one of these groups: the Jews, the Gentiles, or the Church (also known in the Bible as the Body of Christ).

The first group mentioned is the Jewish nation—those whom God chose to set apart as a nation unto Himself, through whom He would bring the Messiah, and with whom He has a natural covenant by way of Abraham. Here the word "Jew" is used in the generic sense as it has come to apply to all of the children of Israel, not just the Judean people around Jerusalem, that is, the tribe of Judah. The second group He recognizes is the Gentiles—those who are not Jewish, and who are not in covenant with Him. The third group is called the Church—and it is made up of both Jews and Gentiles who have accepted Christ as their Savior and who, through Christ, have a spiritual covenant with God.

From the beginning of creation until the end of this world, God has seen all of humanity as being members of one of these three groups. For all the ages of human history, God has had a plan in the center of His heart that includes the third group, the Church. He created mankind, and then chose Abraham to begin the Jewish race—which brought forth the Messiah so that the Church could come into existence. In the Bible, the New Testament calls this "the mystery." And this mystery that God has now revealed to us, through Christ, is at the heart of our authority in Him.

The Role of the Church in God's Plan

This mystery that God has placed at the heart of His plan for the world was hidden from the Old Testament saints and was not revealed until after Jesus came. We will consider why this mystery was hidden until Christ's work on the Cross a little later in this chapter. For now, let us examine what the Apostle Paul said about this mystery in the book of Colossians.

> **Colossians 1:25–27**
>
> *Whereof I am made a minister, according to the dispensation of God which is given to me for you, to fulfil the word of God;*
>
> *Even the mystery which hath been hid from ages and from generations, but now is made manifest to His saints:*
>
> *To whom God would make known what is the riches of the glory of this mystery among the Gentiles; which is Christ in you, the hope of glory.*

In this passage, Paul reveals to us what this mystery is—Christ in us, the hope of glory! For millennia, God has been waiting to bring this revelation into the Earth—that Christ would live inside of His people. And now He does!

To learn more about this mystery of Christ in us, let's look at a passage in the book of Ephesians.

> **Ephesians 3:1–11**
>
> *For this cause I Paul, the prisoner of Jesus Christ for you Gentiles,*
>
> *If ye have heard of the dispensation of the grace of God which is given me to you-ward:*
>
> *How that by revelation He made known unto me the mystery; (as I wrote afore in few words,*
>
> *Whereby, when ye read, ye may understand my knowledge in the mystery of Christ)*
>
> *Which in other ages was not made known unto the sons of men, as it is now revealed unto His holy apostles and prophets by the Spirit;*
>
> *That the Gentiles should be fellow heirs, and of the same body, and partakers of His promise in Christ by the Gospel:*
>
> *Whereof I was made a minister, according to the gift of the grace of God given unto me by the effectual working of His power.*
>
> *Unto me, who am less than the least of all saints, is this grace given, that I should preach among the Gentiles the unsearchable riches of Christ;*
>
> *And to make all men see what is the fellowship of the mystery, which from the beginning of the world hath been hid in God, who created all things by Jesus Christ:*
>
> *To the intent that now unto the principalities and powers in heavenly places might be known by the Church the manifold wisdom of God,*
>
> *According to the eternal purpose which He purposed in Christ Jesus our Lord.*

In verse 6, Paul explains what "the mystery" is. It is that believing Gentiles should be fellow heirs alongside believing Israel. All who believed in Christ would become fellow heirs and members of the same body—the Body of Christ, the Church. And they would share in the promise God made to Abraham—that He would send a Savior to redeem people to Himself. The promise is Jesus Christ. The mystery is that we believers are one with Christ, are in Christ, and are fellow heirs of all that Christ has obtained for us through His death and resurrection.

When considering these passages of Colossians and Ephesians, it is important to note that they are parallel passages. Both of these letters were written by Paul around the same time. There are many similarities between the two letters. For example, Ephesians 5:19 instructs: *Speak to yourselves in psalms and hymns and spiritual songs, singing and making melody in your heart to the Lord.* The parallel passage in Colossians 3:16 says: *Let the word of Christ dwell in you richly in all wisdom; teaching and admonishing one another in psalms and hymns and spiritual songs, singing with grace in your hearts to the Lord.*

The similar topics and thoughts in each book tells us we are to consider these two books connected in terms of what they are revealing to us about God's plans and purposes. We should therefore look at both books in terms of what they tell us about the mystery, so we can gain a fuller understanding of what God is saying.

In Colossians, Paul says the mystery is *Christ in us, the hope of glory*, while in Ephesians, he says it is that *we are in Christ; we are members of His Body.* In Ephesians 3:2–6, Paul offers further details, helping us to see why it is so important for us to understand this mystery if we are to walk in the authority God has given us in Christ. This passage in Ephesians chapter 3 reveals that the mystery is that both Jews and Gentiles would be joined together in one body, the Body of Christ.

This was part of the plan of God that the Old Testament saints didn't understand. They were unaware that God intended to create a people in whom He would dwell and who would dwell in Him.

This plan of God to create the Church was hidden until Christ came, for had the Old Testament saints known the plan of God, it would have become common knowledge. And that means it would have been revealed to the devil, who would have tried to interfere and prevent it from coming to pass. So God, in His wisdom, kept His intention secret to create the Church and give us authority through Christ until after Christ had risen from the dead.

Yet now, the mystery is revealed to all people. We are in Christ, and He is in us. We are seated with Him in heavenly places (Ephesians 2:6). We who are believers in Jesus are a new spiritual race of people—the Body of Christ.

Colossians 2:16–17 says, *Let no man therefore judge you in meat, or in drink, or in respect of an holy day, or of the new moon, or of the sabbath days: which are a shadow of things to come; but the Body is of Christ.* Just as a person walking down the street in sunlight casts a shadow, so does the Old Testament cast a shadow of what was coming: the Body of Christ. We do not live in the shadow anymore. We live in His Body!

Think about how a shadow works. When you look at a person's shadow, you can see arms and legs and a torso and head. You can tell it is a reflection of a person. But you can't describe the person's hair color, or eye color, or choice of clothing from looking at the shadow. A shadow gives us a sense of the shape of something, but it also leaves much information out. It's incomplete.

It is the same with the Old Testament (the shadow) and the New

Testament and Christ (the object which casts the shadow). The Law of Moses and its rules and regulations, the Prophets, and the Writings of the Old Testament were merely a taste of the things to come. They were not the whole picture, any more than a shadow gives you the full picture of the person who casts it. We get the full picture of God's plan only through His Son, Jesus Christ.

From God's viewpoint, at the center of history stands the One who hung on the Cross at Mount Calvary. Not only is Christ's death and resurrection located at the center of history, but geographically Mount Calvary is also in the center of Israel, and Israel is the center of the nations. From the beginning of creation, God has worked His plan to bring the Body of Christ into the Earth. History is really "His story"—God's story of the redemption of man through His Son, Jesus.

Everything in the Old Testament looked toward the Cross, and now everything looks back to that moment in history. At the Cross, at Jesus' death, burial and resurrection, God brought the Body of Christ, or the Church, into existence. At the same time, He brought salvation to the world. This mystery was God's purpose from the beginning! And now that Christ has come, and the Body of Christ is revealed, the shadow is no longer important. We have the real thing. In fact, we *are* the real thing. We are the Body of Christ, and we are one with Him!

Let's consider how important the Church is to God. First Corinthians 3:21–23 says, *Therefore let no man glory in men. For all things are yours; whether Paul, or Apollos, or Cephas, or the world, or life, or death, or things present, or things to come; all are yours; and ye are Christ's; and Christ is God's.*

Notice that in this passage the Holy Spirit, through Paul, says, "All things are yours." We belong to Christ, and Christ belongs to God.

We are in Him, and He is in us. Christ is seated at the right hand of God, and He rules over all things. That means that, through Christ, all things are ours! The world, life and death itself, things present and things to come all belong to us because we are in the Body of Christ.

God also tells us in Romans 8:28, *We are called according to His purpose.* This further confirms how important the Church is to God. He has a purpose for us to fulfill as we walk this Earth. And to fulfill this purpose, we must operate in His authority and power.

Members of the Body of Christ

1 Corinthians 12:12–14

For as the body is one, and hath many members, and all the members of that one body, being many, are one body: so also is Christ.

For by one Spirit are we all baptized into one Body, whether we be Jews or Gentiles, whether we be bond or free; and have been all made to drink into one Spirit.

For the Body is not one member, but many.

Whether Jew or Gentile, when we are born again, we are baptized by the Spirit into the Body of Christ. Paul is talking about the Holy Spirit baptizing us into Jesus, or into the Body of Christ. This happens when we are born again; we become part of His Body. (It is not to be confused with the baptism *in* the Holy Spirit, which is when we receive power for service in the Kingdom of God.) When He was raised from the dead, we were in Him. We were in Him when He conquered the devil, and when He ascended on high, taking His place in the heavenlies (Ephesians 1:15–2:9).

Matthew 7:13-14 says, *Enter ye in at the strait gate: for wide is the gate, and broad is the way, that leadeth to destruction, and many there be which go in thereat: Because strait is the gate, and narrow is the way, which leadeth unto life, and few there be that find it.* In this verse, Jesus said there would be few who would find eternal life with God through faith in Him.

Currently, statistics report that nearly one-third of the world's population is Christian, or about 2.2 billion people. Of course, we know that not everyone who claims to be a Christian is truly a Christian. But with the total world population at approximately 7.6 billion as I write this book, 2.2 billion Christians is still only a few.

Knowing that only a few would be saved, God still sent Jesus to die for us, because we are extremely important to Him. You see, God had a plan—the mystery. He was looking for the Body of Christ. The shadow was already there, but He was looking for the real thing.

> **Matthew 13:44–46**
>
> *Again, the Kingdom of heaven is like unto treasure hid in a field; the which when a man hath found, he hideth, and for joy thereof goeth and selleth all that he hath, and buyeth that field.*
>
> *Again, the Kingdom of heaven is like unto a merchant man, seeking goodly pearls:*
>
> *Who, when he had found one pearl of great price, went and sold all that he had, and bought it.*

This story is another illustration revealing how important the Church is to God. He places great value on the Church, and that means you!

In these verses, God compares the Kingdom of heaven to a treasure hidden in a field. The man who finds this treasure is overjoyed and goes quickly, taking everything he has to buy the entire field because he knows the value of the treasure that lies within it. That's what God did. He spent everything He had to redeem the whole world, even though He knew only a few would receive Him. As far as God was concerned, the number of people who would receive Him compared to those who wouldn't didn't matter. He did what He did for the treasure He'd receive: the Church. God works among the nations on one hand and the Jewish people on the other hand, but everything that takes place in those realms is for the Church. The Church is His prized possession. We are the treasure that God was waiting for. We are at the center of God's attention. He bought the whole world so He could redeem us out of it.

We must realize that the "Church" is not an organization, a denomination, a corporation, or an institution; nor is it a building, cathedral, or place. The Church is Christ's Body on Earth—made up of those who believe in Him and follow Him. He alone is the Head of the Church—not a man.

Colossians 1:18
And He is the head of the Body, the Church: who is the beginning, the firstborn from the dead; that in all things He might have the preeminence.

Ephesians 1:22–23
And hath put all things under His feet, and gave Him to be the head over all things to the Church,

Which is His Body, the fulness of Him that filleth all in all.

It is unfortunate that throughout Church history, much evil has been done by the so-called "church" which had nothing to do with Jesus Christ or His message and ministry.

The separation between those who are in the Church (in Christ) and those who are not is evident in many ways. In the early 1900s, for example, there was a revival in India, and many people received Christ. When this happened, they were rejected from their castes, or family groups. They became their own caste, and to this day, other castes treat them like dirt. They are considered the lowest of the low because they are Christians.

This rejection by the world has happened to the Church in many different ways and in many different cultures. Humans who don't believe in Jesus often reject those who do. Yet it ultimately does not matter what the eyes of man see when they see the Church, because in the eyes of God, we are the treasure of the Earth. The center of His attention is on us. We are His people. We are at the center of His will, and we are "what is happening" in the Earth. Everything that happens in the world is about us, or revolves around this treasure of God—Christ in us, the hope of glory.

> **Colossians 1:15–17**
>
> *Who is the image of the invisible God, the firstborn of every creature:*
>
> *For by Him were all things created, that are in heaven, and that are in Earth, visible and invisible, whether they be thrones, or dominions, or principalities, or powers: all things were created by Him, and for Him:*
>
> *And He is before all things, and by Him all things consist.*

In the beginning, Jesus, as the Word of God, was involved in creation. He created the very principalities and powers that are now under His feet. The devil and all the fallen angels who rebelled against God and were cast out of Heaven were created by Jesus—and He has authority over them.

The following verse, Colossians 1:18, says, *And He is the head of the Body, the Church: who is the beginning, the firstborn from the dead; that in all things He might have the preeminence.* Remember, Christ is the head of the Body. We are that Body, and we are literally one with Him. This means that we are united with the One who both created the devil and then cast him out of Heaven when he rebelled against God. We are one with He who rose from the dead and put the devil under His feet. We are one Body and one with Christ, who is the head of that Body.

The devil is and should be nervous when we are around, because we are united with the head, Christ, his conqueror, his master. The Word of God proclaims, *Greater is He that is in you, than he that is in the world* (1 John 4:4). Jesus is greater than the devil and anything he can do. And as part of His Body, we can tap into Jesus' power and authority to defeat the devil when he tries to cause trouble in our lives.

Coming to Mount Zion

As we mentioned previously, the Old Testament represented a shadow of what was to come in Christ. Even the sacrifices made by the Old Testament saints represented a shadow of the ultimate sacrifice Jesus made on the Cross for us. In Hebrews chapter 11, the writer lists many of the Old Testament saints who had a testimony of faith. They all looked forward to the time when Jesus would come, but never actually saw it during their lifetimes.

Hebrews 11:39–40 says, *And these all, having obtained a good report through faith, received not the promise: God having provided some better thing for us, that they without us should not be made perfect.* Moses and Abraham and all the Old Testament saints who had a testimony of faith did not receive in their lifetime the promised deliverance from sin and authority over the devil that Jesus obtained. Since Jesus hadn't come, they couldn't totally receive what they were waiting for. But now that Christ has come and set us free from the power of sin and death, the Scriptures tell us that God has provided something better for us in our lifetime than what the Old Testament saints had. Without us, the promises God gave them would not be completed.

> **Hebrews 12:18–24**
>
> *For ye are not come unto the mount that might be touched, and that burned with fire, nor unto blackness, and darkness, and tempest,*
>
> *And the sound of a trumpet, and the voice of words; which voice they that heard intreated that the word should not be spoken to them any more:*
>
> *(For they could not endure that which was commanded, And if so much as a beast touch the mountain, it shall be stoned, or thrust through with a dart:*
>
> *And so terrible was the sight, that Moses said, I exceedingly fear and quake:)*
>
> *But ye are come unto mount Sion, and unto the city of the living God, the heavenly Jerusalem, and to an innumerable company of angels,*
>
> *To the general assembly and Church of the firstborn, which are written in Heaven, and to God the Judge of all, and to the spirits of just men made perfect,*
>
> *And to Jesus the mediator of the new covenant, and to the blood of sprinkling, that speaketh better things than that of Abel.*

Verse 22 reveals that, unlike the situation in the Old Testament, we have *already* come to Mount Zion. It does not say that we will go to Mount Zion (Isaiah 2:3, Micah 4:2), but that we are already there. What is Mount Zion? It is the city of the living God, the New Jerusalem, where there are millions of angels and where Jesus is seated at God's right hand. Ephesians tells us that we are seated in heavenly places (Ephesians 2:6), which means that we are seated before the throne of God with all the multitudes of angels and saints. Just think—when we enter into heavenly worship, we are taking part with those who are gathered around the throne of God.

Now, let's examine who else is with the angels around the throne. Verse 23 reveals that the general assembly and the Church of the first-born are also gathered there, in God's presence. This is the Church of God described in 1 Corinthians 10:32, and it includes those who are here with us now as well as those who have gone on before. This verse shows us that God, the judge of all, is there too. It tells us that the spirits of *just men made perfect* are also there. The word *perfect* in this context means to be made complete. Therefore, the spirits of just men made perfect are all of the Old Testament saints.

Before Jesus was raised from the dead, they had been waiting in Abraham's bosom (a place set aside for them after death) for Jesus to rise from the dead, take captivity captive, and usher them into the heavens (Ephesians 4:8). The Old Testament saints could not have been made perfect, or complete in God, until after the resurrection and the Church came into existence. At this moment in the heavens, the Church of the first-born and all of the Old Testament saints who were made complete are present and waiting for us.

In John 8:56, Jesus said, *Your father Abraham rejoiced to see My day: and he saw it, and was glad*. Abraham rejoiced as he saw into the future to the Cross and the day Jesus would come. All of the Old Testament's great men and women of faith were waiting for the death, burial, and resurrection of Jesus to make a way for them to go into Heaven and be with God in person. Before Jesus was resurrected, men went to paradise instead of heaven. And while paradise was pleasant, it still didn't offer the fullness of what is available to us through Christ. So, these saints of God who preceded us in death were waiting for the formation of the Church, and the resurrection of Jesus to be set free and released into Heaven, where they are now complete in God. Even they were amazed to see the mystery that God would create a race of spiritual, supernatural people born of the Spirit, one with Jesus, who would rule and reign with Him.

Since the Cross, we don't need to look forward to and wait for Christ's sacrifice. Today, when we accept Jesus into our hearts as Lord and Savior, we no longer need to look forward to a hope of salvation coming someday. Rather, we look back to the Cross and the completed work of Christ. Our salvation, our righteousness, our healing, and our deliverance are all in our past! They have already happened. We can now enjoy them, by faith.

History and the Church

All of humanity's history before the Cross was centered around how the nations would affect the coming Church. God lined up the nations to suit His purposes and plan for mankind. For this reason, He also created a new nation called Israel, which arose despite many different tribulations, including a struggle to escape slavery from Egypt. He brought the Israelites—the descendants of Abraham, Isaac, and Jacob—through many struggles, fights, enemy attacks, and periods dur-

THE CHURCH FROM GOD'S PERSPECTIVE

ing which they wandered far from God and then repented—all to get them into position so that He could bring forth through them Jesus, the Messiah. He was the One who had to come to buy the pearl, the treasure, in the field that is the world (Matthew 13:44–46), by giving His life so that God could redeem mankind out of the Earth.

From God's perspective, therefore, all of history since the Cross, some 2,000 years, has been centered around how the message of the Gospel has affected the nations. We are writing history right now, as we follow Christ day to day. The Church is affecting the world. History is being written based on how that Body of Believers in Jesus, going forth in the power of the Holy Spirit, affects the nations. Ever since the Church was born, wherever Christianity has spread, it has brought enlightenment into God's Word. In many places, it has produced a higher standard of living. We can look at modernized countries today and see that, even though many of them have forgotten their Christian roots, their prosperity is often rooted in the effect that the Church has had upon them.

Even now, Christianity continues to spread and influence the nations. Although traditional church attendance in Europe and America had been in decline in recent years and replaced by New Age thought and materialism, it is growing in other places. In almost the entire world, the Body of Christ is expanding at a phenomenal rate—faster than the population growth rate.[2]

The Church of God is not dead. It will never be dead. Christianity is not a dead religion. It continues to have a powerful influence on the nations. Even in places like Europe and America, I believe the Church will experience a revival. I believe that if Jesus does not return for another generation, we will see changes continue to happen around the

---
2 Operation World. (n.d.). Retrieved from http://www.operationworld.org/.

world because His Church will continue to affect the history of the nations. We will see prosperity coming into them, great Christian leaders coming out of them, and great churches rising up within them. The Body of Christ is God's priority—through it, He is writing history and changing nations wherever His Church thrives.

The Bill Has Been Paid in Full

Acts 17:26–31
And hath made of one blood all nations of men for to dwell on all the face of the Earth, and hath determined the times before appointed, and the bounds of their habitation;

That they should seek the Lord, if haply they might feel after Him, and find Him, though He be not far from every one of us:

For in Him we live, and move, and have our being; as certain also of your own poets have said, For we are also His offspring.

Forasmuch then as we are the offspring of God, we ought not to think that the Godhead is like unto gold, or silver, or stone, graven by art and man's device.

And the times of this ignorance God winked at; but now commandeth all men every where to repent:

Because He hath appointed a day, in the which He will judge the world in righteousness by that man whom He hath ordained; whereof He hath given assurance unto all men, in that He hath raised Him from the dead.

This passage of Scripture says that God *winked at ignorance* in past times, choosing to overlook some things because people were ignorant of His full plan, His promises, and the mystery of Christ in us. He chose deliberately to grant mercy in this way, because He knew that the price of sin had not yet been paid by Jesus' sacrifice on the Cross. He is much like a patient creditor who isn't worried about a debt because He knows it will eventually be paid.

Thus, when the people of the Old Testament put their faith in God, He accepted their faith as righteousness—as right-standing with Him, owing no debt to Him, even though they were not yet made righteous by Christ's sacrifice. One might say they were saved by credit. For instance, when we use credit to buy something, we are exchanging goods for a promise that we will pay later. Likewise, when the people of the Old Testament put their faith in the sacrifices made at the temple in Jerusalem, they were acquiring righteousness at that moment, knowing that it would be charged to a bill being paid later. Then Jesus came, paid the bill in full, and tore up the debt.

Today, we don't become redeemed, blood-bought Christians by looking forward to a redemption that has yet to occur; we are saved by looking back at the Cross, knowing what we see is "paid in full." This is why God does not overlook ignorance today, as He did before Christ came. There is no other way to obtain forgiveness than through coming to a saving knowledge of Christ. All that took place under the Old Covenant—the sins and the sacrifices that covered them—was paid off and done away with. Today, the only way people can be saved is by looking back to Jesus and the Cross.

The New Jerusalem

In Acts chapter 17, we find an account of the Apostle Paul coming to Thessalonica and preaching there. Certain unbelieving Jews turned the city against Paul. When the Jews brought Paul's friends to the rulers of the city, they cried out, *These that have turned the world upside down are come hither also* (v. 6).

Wherever the Church goes today, we are turning the world upside down. Jesus said that we are the salt of the Earth (Matthew 5:13). Salt is a preserving agent that prevents decay. If it were not for the presence of the Body of Christ in the world today, the Earth would be rotten to the core. But because of the Church, the Earth is preserved.

One day, the Earth as we know it will be placed fully into the hands of Jesus. He will rule and reign over the Earth, with the Church at His side. God's mind and attention are on the Church. The Church is His first priority. God had a plan for the Church—to be forever joined as One with His Son and to rule with Him.

This role is the central purpose of the Church. God intends for us to be a people, created by Him, to be a Bride for His Son. We see this purpose coming to pass in a prophecy shared in Revelation 21:2–3.

> *And I John saw the holy city, new Jerusalem, coming down from God out of heaven, prepared as a bride adorned for her husband.*
>
> *And I heard a great voice out of heaven saying, Behold, the tabernacle of God is with men, and He will dwell with them, and they shall be His people, and God Himself shall be with them, and be their God.*

What makes a city a city is the *people* who live in the city. A city is not a city without people living in it. If nobody lived in New York City, it wouldn't be a city; it would only be a ghost town. And what makes the new Jerusalem are the people who live there. As we saw in Hebrews 12, we, the Church, are in that city. We are the inhabitants of the city, and we are the source of its life.

In Matthew 5:14, Jesus said we are a city on a hill that cannot be hidden because of the light that shines out from it. The Church is the city on a hill. The Church inhabits the new Jerusalem. There is a physical city called new Jerusalem, and it is the inhabitants of the city that make the city what it is.

Let me remind you that the Church is not an organization of man, but a called-out Body of Believers in the Messiah — Jesus Christ.

> **Revelation 21:9–10**
> *And there came unto me one of the seven angels which had the seven vials full of the seven last plagues, and talked with me, saying, Come hither, I will shew thee the Bride, the Lamb's wife.*
>
> *And he carried me away in the spirit to a great and high mountain, and shewed me that great city, the holy Jerusalem, descending out of Heaven from God.*

The end of all current history is going to occur when the Bride of Christ is joined with the Lamb. God will be forever joined with His people and never separated again. We are spiritually joined to Him right now, but the Bible says that when we see Him someday, our mortal bodies will be changed. Then, we shall be like Him (1 John 3:2).

Joined with Him as the Bride of Christ

In Ephesians chapter 5, the Apostle Paul compares the marital relation of a husband and a wife with the relationship between Christ and His Church. The depiction of marriage in the Bible is really a picture of what God plans to do with Christ and the Church.

There are similarities between the Jewish marriage custom and Christ and the Church. In Israel, when a couple intended to get married, the two families would get together. An agreement would be made, and a contract would be signed. The bridegroom would then go away to his father's house, and begin to construct a house where his new bride would live. The time between when they signed the contract and when the bridegroom was going to come back and get his bride could be a year or more. During that time, they were considered engaged.[3]

So in the Jewish custom, during that period of waiting for the bridegroom to return, a bride was considered as belonging to that man, even though the marriage had not yet taken place. A dowry had been paid for the bride; the contract was signed. The bridegroom went to build a home for his new wife. Then on a day when they would not expect to see him, he would come with a processional, blowing a trumpet and shouting, "The bridegroom is coming." The bride would quickly get herself ready, and the bridegroom would come and take her away and go back to his father's house.

Paul paints a picture of the relationship between Christ and the Church in that same way. Like a bridegroom, Jesus came into this world, paid the price for us, and signed the contract. And He told us in John 14:3, *And if I go and prepare a place for you, I will come again, and receive you unto myself; that where I am, there ye may be also.* Right now, Jesus is at His father's house, preparing a place for the Church. We are considered married to Him because we are engaged, and a contract has been signed. Paul describes this state of engagement between the Church and Christ as being *one spirit with the Lord*. We are one with Him, and our lives are to reflect that union.

---

[3] Levitt, Z. (1978). A Christian love story. Dallas, TX: Zola Levitt Publishing.

We Are the Body *and* Bride of Christ

1 Corinthians 6:15–17
Know ye not that your bodies are the members of Christ? shall I then take the members of Christ, and make them the members of an harlot? God forbid.

What? know ye not that he which is joined to an harlot is one body? for two, saith he, shall be one flesh.

But he that is joined unto the Lord is one spirit.

We are members of Christ, a part of His very Body. However, the Bible also calls us the "Bride of Christ." How can we be both the Body of Christ and the Bride of Christ?

Genesis 2:24
Therefore shall a man leave his father and his mother, and shall cleave unto his wife: and they shall be one flesh.

The Bible says that in marriage, two shall become one flesh. In marriage, we do not act alone, but we act as one. As believers, we are not only the Body of Jesus, but also the Church joined unto Him as one flesh. In the natural realm, marriage is just the picture of that which takes place in the spiritual realm. It is a picture of the overall plan of God for the Body of Christ to be changed to be like Him, and to be forever joined spiritually and physically to Him. Jesus told us that in Heaven there will be no more marriage, but we shall be as the angels, in a spiritual condition. The spiritual marriage between Christ and the

Church will have taken place, and there will be no more need for that which is merely a shadow of that reality.

> **Ephesians 5:22–32**
>
> *Wives, submit yourselves unto your own husbands, as unto the Lord.*
>
> *For the husband is the head of the wife, even as Christ is the head of the Church: and he is the saviour of the Body.*
>
> *Therefore as the Church is subject unto Christ, so let the wives be to their own husbands in every thing.*
>
> *Husbands, love your wives, even as Christ also loved the Church, and gave Himself for it;*
>
> *That he might sanctify and cleanse it with the washing of water by the word,*
>
> *That he might present it to Himself a glorious Church, not having spot, or wrinkle, or any such thing; but that it should be holy and without blemish.*
>
> *So ought men to love their wives as their own bodies. He that loveth his wife loveth himself.*
>
> *For no man ever yet hated his own flesh; but nourisheth and cherisheth it, even as the Lord the Church:*
>
> *For we are members of His Body, of His flesh, and of His bones.*
>
> *For this cause shall a man leave his father and mother, and shall be joined unto his wife, and they two shall be one flesh.*
>
> *This is a great mystery: but I speak concerning Christ and the Church.*

In this example of marriage, the way that the woman submits to the husband is a picture of the Church submitting to Christ, and the way that the husband is to love and care for the wife is a picture of Christ taking care of the Church. In verse 31, Paul quotes Genesis 2:24, which says a man and a woman would become one flesh. In verse 32, he says, "This is a mystery, but I'm talking about Christ and the Church." Again, the mystery is Christ in us and us in Christ—the union between Jesus and believers that occurs in the spiritual realm.

In the Gospel of John, Jesus said that He and the Father are one (John 17:21). He also said that He is in us, and we are in Him. You are in Him, and He is in you. It is a great mystery, but we are one with Him.

What is the ultimate purpose of all that God has in mind? Throughout history, since before the Cross until the end of the book of Revelation, He saw the end result and grand finale of Christ's work as the marriage between the Lamb and His wife, the Church.

The Church is therefore very important to God. The relationship that we have with our Lord is like a godly marriage relationship between a human husband and human wife. There should be a mutual submission to one another; the wife respects and trusts her husband, and the husband loves and cares for his wife. The same is true in our relationship with Jesus. We submit to and trust Him, and He loves and takes care of us.

This mutual connection between Christ and His Church is the vehicle through which God's power is manifested in the Earth today. Healings, salvations, and other miracles, as well as the spread of the Gospel to all people, cannot happen if the Church does not do its part. As John Wesley, a founder of Methodism, is often quoted as saying, "Without Him, we cannot. Without us, He will not."

God wants to use us. We are joined together as one with Christ. God executes His will in the Earth through the Church. We can do nothing without Him, and He will do nothing except through us. As head of the Church, Jesus said that all authority in Heaven and in Earth had been given to Him. He then told His disciples to take His message and make disciples of every nation (Matthew 28:19–20). Everything God does in the Earth, He does through Jesus Christ and us, His Body.

Reigning Together

Let's look again at God's plan. He desires a people who can rule and reign together with Him. Second Timothy 2:12 says, *If we suffer, we shall also reign with Him: if we deny Him, He also will deny us.* God's desire is that we reign with Him. Revelation 20:6 says, *Blessed and holy is he that hath part in the first resurrection: on such the second death hath no power, but they shall be priests of God and of Christ, and shall reign with Him a thousand years.* The word *reign* used here means to exercise kingly power.

Revelation 2:10 says, *Fear none of those things which thou shalt suffer: behold, the devil shall cast some of you into prison, that ye may be tried; and ye shall have tribulation ten days: be thou faithful unto death, and I will give thee a crown of life.* In chapters 2 and 3 of the book of Revelation, we find several references to our kingly role. In the verse quoted above, the Lord says that if we overcome, He will give us *a crown of life.*

In Revelation chapters 2 and 3, the Lord is talking to seven churches. Each of these seven short letters within the book of Revelation ends the same way, saying, *To him that overcomes…* Then the Lord states a promise associated with overcoming. You see, God wants overcomers in His family. He wants people who will rule and reign with Him.

Revelation 2:26 says, *And he that overcometh, and keepeth My works unto the end, to him will I give power over the nations.* God is training us to reign with Him. He wants to give us authority over the nations! It is time for us to get serious about serving Him, because as we do so, we will walk in His authority and carry His power and light to places where they are needed.

If you are still not sure about God's desire to give you authority to reign over the devil, look at Revelation 3:21. This verse says, *To him that overcometh will I grant to sit with Me in My throne, even as I also overcame, and am set down with My Father in His throne.* When we overcome, we will reign with Him.

The Bible begins and ends with a man and a woman joined together in a garden, ruling and reigning together with God. In Genesis, God created the Earth and put a garden in it. He then created man and gave him authority over the garden. When God saw that it was not good for Adam to be alone, He created Eve to be Adam's bride and to rule with him in the garden and over the whole Earth. In Revelation 22:1–2, the Bible ends in a garden in a paradise with the marriage of the Lamb and the Bride who will rule over all creation together! Jesus desires to rule the creation of God with His Church.

The Last and First Adam

The Bible tells us that Jesus is the last Adam (1 Corinthians 15:45). As such, He gave birth to a new race that would one day reign over the Earth, just as God intended the first Adam, the man placed in the Garden of Eden in Genesis chapter 1, to do. Let's look closer at these parallels between Genesis and Revelation.

As recorded in Genesis 1:28, God gave the first Adam authority to rule over creation. While Adam slept, God created Eve, his wife and bride, to rule together with Adam. They were given authority over everything in the garden except for a single tree—the tree of the knowledge of good and evil. Of that one tree, they were not to eat, according to God's instructions (Genesis 2:16–17).

Adam and Eve were tempted to disobey this command when the serpent came to them. Genesis 3:6 says, *And when the woman saw that the tree was good for food, and that it was pleasant to the eyes, and a tree to be desired to make one wise, she took of the fruit thereof, and did eat, and gave also unto her husband with her; and he did eat.* Usually, Eve gets the blame for getting mankind into the mess of sin we now find ourselves in. But as we see, Adam was there with her, and he ate too.

What was he doing? What was he thinking? He certainly wasn't doing his job. God had given him authority over the garden, all creation, and the beasts of the field which included the serpent. Adam didn't use his authority. Instead, he just stood there, allowed his wife to be talked into sin by the devil, and then joined right in.

Let's get a better understanding of temptation and look more closely at the three ways Adam and Eve were tempted, because it will show us why it matters for us to be in Christ and how we are to exercise our authority over the devil.

First John 2:15–16 says, *Love not the world, neither the things that are in the world. If any man love the world, the love of the Father is not in him. For all that is in the world, the lust of the flesh, and the lust of the eyes, and the pride of life, is not of the Father, but is of the world.* According to this section of Scripture, all sin falls into one of three categories: the lust of the flesh, the lust of the eyes, and the pride of life. Notice that Adam and Eve were tempted in all three ways. The first was the lust of the flesh; Eve saw that the tree was good for food. The second was the lust of the eyes; it was pleasant to behold. And the third was the pride of life; the tree was desirable to make one wise.

By giving in to the temptation to disobey God, the first Adam, and Eve, failed the test of trusting and obeying God. As a result, they lost their authority over the Earth and the devil. All of their descendants, including us, have been left to struggle with a fallen world and the results of sin that have plagued humanity ever since.

Contrast their temptation and disobedience to the temptation and obedience of the last Adam, Jesus, when He was on the Earth. He was tested the very same way Adam and Eve were tested. In Matthew 4:1–11, He was led by the Spirit into the wilderness where He was tempted with those same three temptations, only in different forms.

Matthew 4:3 says, *And when the tempter came to Him, he said, If Thou be the Son of God, command that these stones be made bread*. At the time, Jesus had been fasting for 40 days and 40 nights when the devil tempted Him. Of course, Jesus was hungry. So, the devil tempted Him with the lusts of the flesh in the same way he tempted Eve and the first Adam.

Jesus had power over earthly things like bread. Later on in His ministry, He would multiply a few loaves of bread into enough to feed 5,000 people. But now, He was fasting for a spiritual purpose. And He refused to break away from that purpose to feed His body until the fast was over. So He resisted the devil by quoting the Scriptures: *It is written, Man shall not live by bread alone, but by every word that proceedeth out of the mouth of God* (Matt. 4:4).

The temptations continue in Matthew 4:5–6: *Then the devil taketh Him up into the holy city, and setteth Him on a pinnacle of the temple, and saith unto Him, If Thou be the Son of God, cast Thyself down: for it is written, He shall give His angels charge concerning Thee: and in their hands they shall bear Thee up, lest at any time Thou dash Thy foot against a stone.*

In this temptation, the devil was appealing to Jesus' pride, saying, "If You really are the Son of God, jump off the temple. Surely the angels will rescue You in a spectacular way. Then, everyone will know that You are the Son of God." Again, Jesus resisted the temptation by quoting God's Word: *It is written again, Thou shalt not tempt the Lord thy God.*

The final attack that the devil launched against Jesus at this time is found in Matthew 4:8–9, which says, *Again, the devil taketh Him up into an exceeding high mountain, and sheweth Him all the kingdoms of the world, and the glory of them; and saith unto Him, All these things will I give Thee, if Thou wilt fall down and worship me.* This temptation was an appeal to the lust of the eyes. The devil showed Him *all the kingdoms of the world, and the glory of them* and said he would give Jesus all these things if He would only fall down and worship the devil.

Now, the devil had authority over the kingdoms of the world because the first Adam, and Eve, forfeited their authority to him when they disobeyed God and obeyed the devil instead. So, in this verse, the devil was offering Jesus a chance to have some authority to rule, if He would submit Himself to the devil. This was essentially what the serpent in the Garden of Eden offered Adam and Eve when he tempted them. They gave in, and they fell from grace that day.

This time, however, the results were different. Jesus refused to submit to the devil. He ordered the devil to leave, saying, *Get thee hence, Satan: for it is written, Thou shalt worship the Lord thy God, and Him only shalt thou serve* (Matt 4:10). He resisted the devil's suggestions and overcame the temptations with the Word of God each time. He didn't give away the authority God had given Him over creation. Instead, Jesus overcame the devil and didn't lose His authority!

The Authority Jesus Had on Earth

How do we know that the last Adam, Jesus, had authority over creation? In Mark 4:35–41, we find the story of Jesus and His disciples crossing the Sea of Galilee when a great storm arose. Jesus was asleep in the back of the boat as the waves battered the ship and began to fill it with water. In sheer panic, His disciples woke Him and said, "Don't You care? We're going to die!"

In response, Jesus stood to His feet and commanded the waves to be still and the wind to cease. Instantly, there was a great calm. His disciples were amazed that the wind and the sea obeyed Him. But Jesus wasn't surprised. He expected the storm to obey Him, because He knew He had authority over it.

At the beginning, in Genesis, Adam had the same authority over the Earth. But he failed the test of faith in God when he disobeyed His word and ate of the tree against God's will. Thus, he lost his authority. Jesus, the last Adam, didn't fail the test. Instead, He used His authority and spoke to creation, and it obeyed Him!

Luke 4:32 (NKJV) says, *And they were astonished at His teaching, for His word was with authority*. Luke 4:36 says, *And they were all amazed, and spake among themselves, saying, What a word is this! For with authority and power He commandeth the unclean spirits, and they come out*. Jesus taught with authority and commanded demons with authority. Jesus had authority in the Earth, and He exercised it with confidence and faith, receiving results every time.

There are more similarities between the first Adam and the last Adam, Jesus, that we should consider in terms of the Church and our authority in Him. While Adam slept, God created a bride to rule with him from a rib taken from his side. When Jesus slept, meaning when He died on the Cross, God created a Bride to rule with Him.

> **John 19:33–35**
>
> *But when they came to Jesus, and saw that He was dead already, they brake not His legs:*
>
> *But one of the soldiers with a spear pierced His side, and forthwith came there out blood and water.*
>
> *And he that saw it bare record, and his record is true: and he knoweth that he saith true, that ye might believe.*

Notice what the Roman soldiers did to Jesus after He had died, or after He was asleep; they pierced His side, and blood and water came out. Acts 20:28 says, *Take heed therefore unto yourselves, and to all the flock, over the which the Holy Ghost hath made you overseers, to feed the Church of God, which He hath purchased with His own blood.* The word *purchase* means to gain or to get for oneself. The blood that flowed out of Jesus' side while He slept in death purchased His Bride. According to Ephesians 5:30–32, that Bride is the Church: *For we are members of His Body, of His flesh, and of His bones. For this cause shall a man leave his father and mother, and shall be joined unto his wife, and they two shall be one flesh. This is a great mystery: but I speak concerning Christ and the Church.* And what is the purpose of the Bride? To rule together with Him!

The Great Exchange

Second Corinthians 5:21 says Jesus, who knew no sin, became sin for us, so that we would become His righteousness. This is called the great exchange. We gave Him our sin, and He gave us His righteousness.

This exchange has many benefits attached to it. One is that we are reconciled to God because of it. Romans 5:11 says, *And not only so, but we also joy in God through our Lord Jesus Christ, by whom we have now received the atonement.* Through our faith in Christ, we receive the reconciliation between ourselves and God. Our sin is paid for. We are no longer debtors, but free to serve God and worship Him in spirit and truth.

Another benefit of the great exchange is our redemption from the curse of the Law. According to Deuteronomy 28, a curse would come upon those who did not fully obey the Law of Moses. Unfortunately, no man can keep the Law in his own strength. No matter how we try to obey God, the sin nature we received through our forefather Adam condemns us to sin too. The ultimate curse of the Law is sin and death—that is, separation from God.

Through His death on the Cross, Jesus solved this problem for us. He paid for our sin, becoming a curse on the Cross in our place (Galatians 3:13). We see this in Hebrews 2:9, which says, *But we see Jesus, who was made a little lower than the angels for the suffering of death, crowned with glory and honour; that He by the grace of God should taste death for every man.* And in Hebrews 2:14, which says, *Forasmuch then as the children are partakers of flesh and blood, He also Himself likewise took part of the same; that through death He might destroy him that had the power of death, that is, the devil.*

Through His death on the Cross, Jesus destroyed the power of the devil. No longer does the devil have full rights to the authority that he gained from Adam and Eve when they served him through sinning against God. Now, that authority rests in Jesus' hands, and thus in the hands of the Church as well. All the devil can do now is deceive others into believing he is in control. He is like a thief without a weapon. Or as the Bible says, he is like a lion who goes about roaring, trying to see who he might devour (1 Peter 5:8). Yet because of Jesus, the devil has no teeth.

As far as the Church is concerned, the devil can only do what we allow him to do. James 4:7 says, *Submit yourselves therefore to God. Resist the devil, and he will flee from you.* As we resist the devil in faith, he must yield to us. We have authority over him, through Christ.

Paul says this mystery was hidden from former generations before him. But it is now revealed to all those who will pay attention to it and receive it. You can see why this revelation of the Church's power over the devil would need to be hidden until Christ fulfilled His purpose on Earth. If the principalities (the demonic forces) of the world knew the plan of God ahead of time, they would have never crucified Jesus. They would not have wanted human beings to be redeemed. They wouldn't have wanted to lose their authority over the Earth. They would have tried to prevent it from happening. This is why God kept it all a secret until the plan had been completed.

1 Corinthians 2:7–8
But we speak the wisdom of God in a mystery, even the hidden wisdom, which God

ordained before the world unto our glory:

Which none of the princes of this world knew: for had they known it, they would not have crucified the Lord of glory.

Now that the plan has been completed, this mystery of God has been made known through the Church. The plan of God no longer remains hidden. We are in Christ, and He is in us. This is the basis of our redemption. And it is the basis for the authority we have over the devil today.

This authority over the devil is something we all have in Christ. It applies to every believer. You may be tempted to say you're not a very important person in the Body of Christ. You may feel like the littlest toe in the Body of Christ. But I want you to know that even the littlest toe in the Body of Christ still has authority over the devil.

All Things Work Together for Our Good

Romans 8:28–29
And we know that all things work together for good to them that love God, to them who are the called according to His purpose.

For whom He did foreknow, He also did predestinate to be conformed to the image of His Son, that He might be the firstborn among many brethren.

This is another reassurance that God's purpose and focus is on the Body of Christ, the Church. God is working all things together for us, for our good. We have a high calling in Christ as members of His Church, His Body, representing Him in the world. We are to enforce

His authority in the world and be a light that reveals Jesus to those who do not yet know Him as Savior and Lord.

When you grab hold of this message and understand what it means to walk in His authority, you can go out and change the world. When you understand who you are in Christ, it will open up a whole world of opportunity for you. God can take you and send you around the world in ministry or business and turn your life around, and you will have what you need to be successful, because you carry His authority with you wherever you go.

Remember, God is looking for anyone who is willing to believe Him for the impossible. And He will take the most unlikely person, the foolish things of this world, to confound the wise and the strong with how He works. As you stick with God, He will continue to move you from level to level to get you where you need to be.

CHAPTER 4

AUTHORITY GIVEN — AUTHORITY LOST

To understand the authority that Jesus gave to us, His Church and His Bride, we must first understand the authority that God gave to the first man, Adam, in the garden of Eden at the dawn of creation. This is the same authority that Adam lost to Satan when he disobeyed God. And it is the same authority that Jesus then won back from Satan through His redemptive work on the Cross.

Let's begin examining this progression of authority given, authority lost, and authority regained with a look at what the Scriptures tell us about man's authority.

Hebrews 2:6–9

But one in a certain place testified, saying, What is man, that thou art mindful of him? or the son of man that thou visitest him?

Thou madest him a little lower than the angels; thou crownedst him with glory and honour, and didst set him over the works of thy hands:

Thou hast put all things in subjection under his feet. For in that he put all in subjection under him, he left nothing that is not put under him. But now we see not yet all things put under him.

But we see Jesus, who was made a little lower than the angels for the suffering of death, crowned with glory and honour; that He by the grace of God should taste death for every man.

In this passage, the writer of Hebrews is referring to Psalm 8, which describes how God gave the first man, Adam, authority over the Earth. But the book of Hebrews goes on to explain that even though God's intention was that man would rule over the Earth, we currently don't see him exercising complete dominion over all that God created and gave to us.

We do, however, see Jesus, the Savior, who was made a little lower than the angels. Jesus tasted death for all of us. He carried the punishment for our sin and died as a cursed man on the cross, though He had never Himself sinned against God. As a result of His righteousness and sinlessness, Jesus conquered the devil and regained the authority that Adam lost. He now has dominion over God's creation.

But, how exactly did Adam lose this God-given dominion over the Earth? And how did the devil gain it?

Man in Charge: God's Original Plan

Before we as believers in Christ can take our place of authority in Him, we must understand what God originally planned for man to do and be. We must go back and look at the creation of the world. And when we do, we see that in the beginning, God gave man complete authority over all the Earth.

Genesis 1:27–28

So God created man in His own image, in the image of God created He him; male and female created He them.

And God blessed them, and God said unto them, Be fruitful, and multiply, and replenish the Earth, and subdue it: and have dominion over the fish of the sea, and over the fowl of the air, and over every living thing that moveth upon the Earth.

Notice what this Scripture reveals to us. First, we learn that human beings were created in the very image of God. Second, we learn that God's original plan was to *bless* humanity. He offered a blessing that included being fruitful and multiplying. And notice that in God's original plan, mankind wasn't just to produce a lot of offspring; we were also intended to subdue the Earth and have dominion over every living thing upon the Earth.

This original plan for human beings was not and is not hidden knowledge. It is something that mankind has been aware of since the beginning of our history. King David, for example, was aware of how the world was created, and what God intended for man to have dominion over. We see this knowledge expressed in Psalm 8.

Psalm 8:3–6

When I consider Thy heavens, the work of Thy fingers, the moon and the stars, which Thou hast ordained;

What is man, that Thou art mindful of him? And the son of man, that Thou visitest him?

For thou hast made him a little lower than the angels, and hast crowned him with glory and honour.

Thou madest him to have dominion over the works of thy hands; Thou hast put all things under his feet.

God's original design was to make all things subject to Adam. God created the world, and then He created man. He set man in the Garden of Eden and said, "Adam, I've created all of this for you. Here are the keys; you're in charge. You are in authority over this Earth. In essence, you are the god of this world because you are in charge of everything I have created."

It's important to understand that when God gave this authority to Adam, He was in essence delegating His authority to man. Human beings were to act on God's behalf in overseeing the Earth. Adam, Eve, and their descendants were intended to rule over the Earth and enact God's will in the Earth, acting as His agents—much like the centurion in Jesus' day was an agent of Rome. Do you recall the centurion who visited Jesus because His servant was sick? Let's look at that as an example of how delegated authority works.

> **Matthew 8:5–13**
>
> *And when Jesus was entered into Capernaum, there came unto Him a centurion, beseeching Him,*
>
> *And saying, Lord, my servant lieth at home sick of the palsy, grievously tormented.*
>
> *And Jesus saith unto him, I will come and heal him.*
>
> *The centurion answered and said, Lord, I am not worthy that Thou shouldest come under my roof: but speak the word only, and my servant shall be healed.*
>
> *For I am a man under authority, having soldiers under me: and I say to this man, Go, and he goeth; and to another, Come, and he cometh; and to my servant, Do this, and*

he doeth it.

When Jesus heard it, He marvelled, and said to them that followed, Verily I say unto you, I have not found so great faith, no, not in Israel.

And I say unto you, That many shall come from the east and west, and shall sit down with Abraham, and Isaac, and Jacob, in the kingdom of heaven.

But the children of the kingdom shall be cast out into outer darkness: there shall be weeping and gnashing of teeth.

And Jesus said unto the centurion, Go thy way; and as thou hast believed, so be it done unto thee. And his servant was healed in the selfsame hour.

Notice that when the centurion comes to ask Jesus to heal his ill servant, Jesus' first response is to say, "Sure, I'll come to your house." In fact, there are many examples of Jesus going to people's homes to heal them, and even spending time in the houses of sinners when He wanted to minister to someone. So, it wouldn't have been in any way unusual for Jesus to go to the centurion's home and pray for the servant in person.

But the centurion doesn't want to do that. He says, "No, I'm not worthy for you to enter my home." What he may have meant was that he was not Jewish. To enter into the house of someone who was a Gentile (a non-Jew) would have potentially caused problems for a Jewish person, who might have been considered unclean for entering a non-Jewish person's home.

Or perhaps the centurion simply felt he didn't deserve a personal visit from Jesus, whom he recognized as having authority greater than his own. Regardless of what was motivating the centurion, however, one thing is certainly true: he understands how delegated authority works, because he himself has been delegated authority by the Emperor in Rome.

As a soldier of Rome in charge of other soldiers, there are certain things that the centurion is authorized to do. He can say to one of his soldiers, "Go," and as soon as he gives the order, the man goes. He can say to another soldier, "Come here," and the man will come. He can say to a servant, "Do this," and the servant will do it.

All these men that the centurion orders to act do so, without question. There are no arguments. There are no consultations. The men just obey, because the centurion has the right to give them orders. He has the right, because the Emperor of Rome, who rules over Rome, has said so. The centurion doesn't simply have authority; he is *under* the authority of another, of one more powerful than he is. When he speaks, he has the full authority of Rome backing him, and all the rewards that come with obeying Rome, and all the punishments that come with disobedience.

The Bible says that Jesus marveled at this centurion's faith, because the man understood the power of delegated authority in a way that many others did not. And by the way, the man's servant was healed at that very hour, because of his faith in God.

But the key point of this passage as it relates to Adam and Eve is this: There was great power available to Adam and Eve, power to rule over the Earth and subdue it, because God had delegated that authority to them. They were to act in His behalf on the Earth. And when they did, the Earth would yield its fruit in season and be productive for them. They would be blessed by using God's authority as He intended, according to His will.

This is why it mattered for Adam and Eve to obey God's instructions concerning all the garden, including the one tree in the garden that He instructed them not to eat of.

> **Genesis 2:16–17**
>
> *And the Lord God commanded the man, saying, Of every tree of the garden thou mayest freely eat:*
>
> *But of the tree of the knowledge of good and evil, thou shalt not eat of it: for in the day that thou eatest thereof thou shalt surely die.*

The whole point of putting one tree in the garden that Adam was not to eat from was to establish a limit to his authority. God had *delegated* a certain degree of authority to Adam, but that didn't mean Adam could do anything he wanted. He was to operate within the limits set by God who had given him the authority to act in His name, on His behalf, just as the centurion was to operate within the limits delegated to him by Rome. The centurion could only do what he was authorized to do. And the same was true of Adam. Adam was only to do what God instructed him to do—no more, and no less.

Tempted to Rebel Against God's Authority

When the devil showed up in the form of a serpent, notice that he didn't invite Adam and Eve to take a swim in the river, or to eat berries from one of the bushes. Why not? Because those were things that Adam and Eve were permitted to do with the authority they'd been given. No, the devil went straight to tempting them to disobey God and act outside of the boundaries of the authority they had been given.

Genesis 3:1–6

Now the serpent was more subtil than any beast of the field which the Lord God had made. And he said unto the woman, Yea, hath God said, Ye shall not eat of every tree of the garden?

And the woman said unto the serpent, We may eat of the fruit of the trees of the garden:

But of the fruit of the tree which is in the midst of the garden, God hath said, Ye shall not eat of it, neither shall ye touch it, lest ye die.

And the serpent said unto the woman, Ye shall not surely die:

For God doth know that in the day ye eat thereof, then your eyes shall be opened, and ye shall be as gods, knowing good and evil.

And when the woman saw that the tree was good for food, and that it was pleasant to the eyes, and a tree to be desired to make one wise, she took of the fruit thereof, and did eat, and gave also unto her husband with her; and he did eat.

In this passage of Scripture, we see that Adam and Eve were tempted to eat of the tree of the knowledge of good and evil, the one tree in the garden that was beyond their authority, according to what God had told them. Now, let's look again at the authority Adam and Eve *did* have.

Genesis 1:28–30

And God blessed them, and God said unto them, Be fruitful, and multiply, and replenish the Earth, and subdue it: and have dominion over the fish of the sea, and over the fowl of the air, and over every living thing that moveth upon the Earth.

And God said, Behold, I have given you every herb bearing seed, which is upon the face of all the Earth, and every tree, in the which is the fruit of a tree yielding seed; to you it shall be for meat.

And to every beast of the Earth, and to every fowl of the air, and to every thing that creepeth upon the Earth, wherein there is life, I have given every green herb for meat: and it was so.

Notice that Adam and Eve had been given authority over all the animals. Isn't it interesting that Genesis 3:1 says the serpent was the craftiest of all the animals? This means that the serpent was created by God. Yet when the serpent came into the garden, Adam and Eve didn't exercise their authority. They should have kicked it out of the garden! Instead, they listened to it and allowed it to suggest that they disobey God and rebel against His authority. Using the serpent, Satan tempted Eve, and Adam did nothing to stop it, even though he could have.

After all, Adam was to keep the garden safe. He had authority over everything that moved upon the Earth. He could have simply said, "Snake, you're telling me to do something God has ordered me not to do. I'm not doing it. Now, get out of here." And the serpent, Satan, would have had to obey. But Adam and Eve both entertained the devil instead. Why?

According to 1 John 2:15–16, all temptation can be broken down into three areas: the lust of the eyes, the lust of the flesh, and the pride of life. The lust of the eyes pertains to desire and covetousness. Some people want whatever they see—cars, houses, and other things. And it is not evil to want cars and houses, as long as you don't seek those things more than God. But when we desire something more than we desire God, or when we allow our desires to drive us to disobey God or hurt others, we are in trouble.

The lusts of the flesh are the desires of your body—hunger, sleep, or sex—which are all natural desires when channeled properly. We are to exercise self-control, according to Galatians 5:23. We are to maintain our body with discipline, because it is a temple of the Holy Spirit, and our body is to be used as a vehicle to glorify God and accomplish His will on Earth. When we allow our desires to get out of control, they become lusts that drive us into sin.

The third area where we are tempted is in the area of pride. This is the very opposite of the humility that Jesus showed when He didn't consider His position in heaven as Son of God so important that He wouldn't come to Earth in the form of a human being to become our Savior. Pride causes us to view ourselves as more important than God, or as being so like God that we can be His equals. It is the sin that caused the devil to desire to take God's throne, leading to his being cast out of heaven.

Adam and Eve were tempted in all three areas by the devil in the Garden. Genesis 3:6 says the tree's fruit was pleasing to Eve's eyes—the lust of the eyes. Also, the passage says that it was good for food—the lust of the flesh. And finally, the fruit would make her wise—the pride of life. And so Eve ate of the tree, and Adam did too.

Unfortunately, Adam as a free moral agent submitted himself to the devil that day and obeyed him. At that moment, Adam became the devil's servant. Romans 6:16 says, *Know ye not, that to whom ye yield yourselves servants to obey, his servants ye are to whom ye obey; whether of sin unto death, or of obedience unto righteousness?* When Adam obeyed the devil, and in so doing disobeyed God, he became the devil's servant. He surrendered his authority to rule and reign over the Earth, and handed that authority over to the devil. At that point, the devil became the god of this world (2 Corinthians 4:4) and gained authority over the Earth.

Adam then became subject to sin, Satan, and death. The result was that all humanity became slaves to the devil. Slaves have no rights; slaves have no authority. They are subject to their master. And Satan has been a cruel master over the entire human race ever since.

The God of This World

So, Adam surrendered the keys to the Earth to the devil, much as you might hand the keys to a car you sell over to its new owner. When this happened, Satan gained control over the world. He could now rule over it and do with it as he pleased, just as Adam was supposed to have done in God's original plan. He became "the god of this world."

> **2 Corinthians 4:3–4**
> *But if our gospel be hid, it is hid to them that are lost:*
>
> *In whom the god of this world hath blinded the minds of them which believe not, lest the light of the glorious gospel of Christ, who is the image of God, should shine unto them.*
>
> **Ephesians 2:2**
> *Wherein in time past ye walked according to the course of this world, according to the prince of the power of the air, the spirit that now worketh in the children of disobedience.*

From the day Adam surrendered the Earth, the devil has been ruling over the world's system. And he is also called the prince of the power of the air, the spirit that works in those who disobey God. This is why we see the works of the devil, and the results of sin, running rampant in the Earth. Disease, poverty, famine, suffering, grief, loss and death are all the result of sin. They are not God's will for us. But the devil happily encourages people to do evil, causing these things to continue and grow worse, because his desire is to ruin God's creation.

The devil's authority over the world system was so complete that when Jesus came to Earth, the devil could literally offer him a chance to reign over all the kingdoms of the Earth at that time. We've already discussed what happened when Satan tempted Jesus, but let's look at the second temptation in terms of the authority the devil took from Adam.

> **Luke 4:5–6**
> *And the devil, taking Him up into an high mountain, shewed unto Him all the kingdoms of the world in a moment of time.*
>
> *And the devil said unto Him, All this power will I give Thee, and the glory of them: for that is delivered unto me; and to whomsoever I will I give it.*

Notice that the devil said a very interesting thing. He said, "All this power You see in the Earth, all these kingdoms, and all their glory, I will give to You if You'll submit to me. They have been *delivered unto me*, so I can give them to whoever I want." How were these kingdoms and their power and glory delivered unto the devil? It happened when Adam gave him the keys to the Earth, his dominion over it. This is what it means when we say that Adam handed his authority over the Earth to the devil due to sin. It was Adam who handed over his authority to Satan—and from that time until Jesus came, all of mankind was Satan's servant.

It is important to understand that the *ownership* of the earth always has, and always will, belong to God: *The earth is the LORD'S, and the fulness thereof; the world, and they that dwell therein.* (Psalm 24:1) It was the *stewardship* and the *authority* of the earth that were delegated to Adam.

God's Plan to Restore Authority to Man

Thankfully, God is merciful, and He was willing to offer mankind a second chance. To bring about this second chance, He already had a plan—a plan that would defeat the devil, return authority over the Earth to humanity, and forgive man's sin. We see the beginning of this restoration plan in Genesis 3, right after Adam's and Eve's disobedience is revealed.

Genesis 3:15
And I will put enmity between thee and the woman, and between thy seed and her seed; it shall bruise thy head, and thou shalt bruise his heel.

This Scripture is the first prophecy in the Bible of the coming of Jesus Christ. Jesus would be "the Seed of Woman." The devil would bruise Jesus' heel—a reference to Jesus' death on the Cross. But Jesus would bruise the devil's head, crushing his power and taking back what he stole from Adam and Eve—a reference to Jesus' resurrection, ascension to heaven, and the birth of the Church as His Body at work in the Earth.

In Genesis 3:21, after God gave Adam and Eve this prophecy, He did something else He had never done before. God made them clothes from animal skins. Why did He do that? When Adam and Eve realized they were naked, they covered themselves with leaves. They sewed leaves together in an effort to cover their own sins.

Did you know that every religion on Earth goes back to this picture? Every religion, except Christianity, is based on man's efforts to deal with our own sin. In some religions, people will even beat themselves, crawl on glass, or perform all kinds of punishments on their bodies to try to pay the price for their wrongdoing. Religions are filled with laws and regulations to deal with humanity's sinful nature. Yet those rules and regulations are just like the fig leaves Adam and Eve tried to use to cover themselves. Using leaves was the best they could do to make things right, but leaves do not make good clothes, and they do not cover our nakedness very well.

So God replaced their fig leaves with animal skins. In doing so, He was showing Adam and Eve that their best efforts were not enough to wash away their sin. Only blood would pay the price for sin, according to Hebrews 9:22—*Without shedding of blood is no remission*. And only innocent blood shed by a man would pay that price for all eternity. The first sacrifice in the Bible happened when two animals had to die and shed their blood to cover Adam and Eve's nakedness. This is a picture of Jesus, the One who was to come and crush the serpent's head.

The Seed of the Woman

Notice that when God promised to send a Savior in Genesis 3:15, He referred to that Savior as *the Seed of the Woman*, not the seed of the man. Why would He not call Jesus the seed of a man? Anyone who knows how a baby is conceived knows that a woman's egg is fertilized by the seed of a man. When the seed of man enters the egg, it carries with it the bloodline of the father. Let me say that again—the male seed carries its bloodline into the child.

Why would God not want to call Jesus the seed of Adam? The answer is simple, yet powerful to our understanding of how Jesus redeemed us, as well as how He won back the authority that Adam surrendered to the devil. To be a Savior who could defeat the devil and restore authority back to mankind, Jesus would have to be born of a woman—having humanity—but He could not be born of a man, because He needed to be born without the sin nature.

In other words, God could not send a Savior who was the seed—or child—of a man, because the first man, Adam, sold all of humanity into sin. If Adam's seed had been used, the child would have been a sinner. The child would have sin in his blood and would not be able to resist the temptation to sin. A child of man would be born a slave to Satan, unable to obey God fully. So, the Savior could not have Adam's blood in His veins.

For this reason, God prophesied about the virgin birth. Why did Jesus have to be born of a virgin? Because Jesus had to have no sin in His bloodline, but He also had to be a human being.

Why couldn't God step down in the midst of everything and take back the authority that Satan had taken from Adam? He couldn't do it that way because He had delegated that authority to Adam and Eve, to do with as they wished. They had the right to do with the Earth as they pleased. God originally created man to have authority over all the Earth. However, Adam lost his authority by obeying Satan and sinning against God. And in sinning, he surrendered the Earth and their rulership of it over to Satan. Man was in charge, and man gave his rulership away.

In a way, it's a lot like receiving a gift from someone we know. If someone buys you a car for a gift, it's your car. It belongs to you, and you can do with it as you wish. You can clean it or let it stay dirty. You can drive it or let it sit. If you don't take care of the car and it breaks down, the person who gave the car to you is not going to come and take it away. The car is yours, so it's your responsibility.

It is the same with Adam and his authority over the Earth. God gave him the right to do anything with the Earth except to eat of the tree of the knowledge of good and evil. Adam ended up giving the Earth over to the devil.

In order for the authority over the Earth to be put back into the proper hands, a human being would need to do the job. Someone would have to come as a man and challenge Satan to get man's authority back. The problem was that every man born after Adam was a slave to sin and to Satan. This is why God said, "I'm going to send the Seed of a Woman, and He's going to crush the devil's head."

The Seed Comes Through Abraham

We have already discussed how God sees three groups of people—the nations, Israel, and the Church. But these groups did not all come into existence at the same time. Before the Church came into being, there were first Israel and the nations. Before Israel, there were just the nations. There were no Israelites before Abraham. Abraham's family were considered Syrians (Genesis 25:20; 28:5; 31:20). He lived in the land of Chaldees, which is modern-day Iraq. He came from the other side of the Euphrates River, which today is known as Iraq, just north of Kuwait.

But God's plan to bring forth the Seed of the Woman to be our Savior also required a nation that would be dedicated to protecting the plan of God until it was the appointed time for the seed to be born. God needed a nation to stand in faith for His promises, a nation that would obey Him, a nation that He would call Israel. But Israel did not yet exist. God had to build that nation. And He started with one man who was willing to stand in faith and believe Him—a man named Abraham.

> **Genesis 12:1–3**
>
> *Now the Lord had said unto Abram, Get thee out of thy country, and from thy kindred, and from thy father's house, unto a land that I will shew thee:*
>
> *And I will make of thee a great nation, and I will bless thee, and make thy name great; and thou shalt be a blessing:*
>
> *And I will bless them that bless thee, and curse him that curseth thee: and in thee shall all families of the Earth be blessed.*

God spoke to Abraham and told him to leave his family and country and go to a place that God would reveal to him. When Abraham obeyed God, God promised him, "I'll give you children. I'll give you seed. And in your offspring, all the Earth will be blessed." This was another reference to the coming of the promised Savior, Jesus.

Abraham believed the promise God made to him. And through his faith, he brought about the beginning a new race of people in the Earth. It was through the faith of Abraham that the Jewish nation was born. When Abraham believed God and it was counted unto him as righteousness, he was no longer an Assyrian, but he became known as the Father of Israel. His faith started a brand-new race of people

IN MY NAME

through Isaac his son, then Jacob the son of Isaac, then the twelve sons of Jacob—whose name was changed to Israel.

> **Romans 4:19–25**
>
> *And being not weak in faith, he considered not his own body now dead, when he was about an hundred years old, neither yet the deadness of Sarah's womb:*
>
> *He staggered not at the promise of God through unbelief; but was strong in faith, giving glory to God;*
>
> *And being fully persuaded that, what he had promised, he was able also to perform.*
>
> *And therefore it was imputed to him for righteousness.*
>
> *Now it was not written for his sake alone, that it was imputed to him;*
>
> *But for us also, to whom it shall be imputed, if we believe on Him that raised up Jesus our Lord from the dead;*
>
> *Who was delivered for our offences, and was raised again for our justification.*

From God's perspective, the faith of Abraham was exercised at two pivotal points in his life. It was first exercised when God promised him that he would have a son. Since both he and Sarah were beyond childbearing age, it took an operation of their faith to supernaturally receive the promise of their son, according to this passage in Romans. Isaac's birth was a miracle of God.

The second pivotal moment of Abraham's faith occurred when God told him to offer up his only son Isaac as a sacrifice. At the time God asked this, Isaac was around 30 to 33 years old.

Hebrews 11:17–19

By faith Abraham, when he was tried, offered up Isaac: and he that had received the promises offered up his only begotten son,

Of whom it was said, That in Isaac shall thy seed be called:

Accounting that God was able to raise him up, even from the dead; from whence also he received him in a figure.

We see here that Abraham had received, by faith, the promise of a son and had to stand in faith to be willing to offer up his son as a sacrifice. In verse 19, we see that by faith, he believed God could even raise up Isaac from the dead if He had to. In fact, the writer of Hebrews says he actually did receive his son back from the dead, in a sense, because by faith, he gave Isaac totally over to the Lord and put his faith in God to receive his son back safely.

Why would God ask Abraham to do that? It was so unusual. The truth is, God never expected Abraham to slay Isaac. He had a plan for a substitute instead.

Genesis 22:8–13

And Abraham said, My son, God will provide Himself a lamb for a burnt offering: so they went both of them together.

And they came to the place which God had told him of; and Abraham built an altar there, and laid the wood in order, and bound Isaac his son, and laid him on the altar upon the wood.

And Abraham stretched forth his hand, and took the knife to slay his son.

And the angel of the Lord called unto him out of heaven, and said, Abraham, Abraham: and he said, Here am I.

And he said, Lay not thine hand upon the lad, neither do thou any thing unto him: for now I know that thou fearest God, seeing thou hast not withheld thy son, thine only son from me.

And Abraham lifted up his eyes, and looked, and behold behind him a ram caught in a thicket by his horns: and Abraham went and took the ram, and offered him up for a burnt offering in the stead of his son.

In this passage of Scripture, we learn that Abraham was trusting God to provide a lamb to take Isaac's place as the sacrifice. And God did indeed have a ram nearby, ready to be sacrificed on the altar. But God waited until the last moment to reveal the ram, because He wanted Abraham to stand in faith for a substitute to be provided. Why? Because God had promised Abraham that through Isaac's offspring, all the nations of the world would be blessed. That blessing would be the coming of our Savior, Jesus Christ.

Whenever God asked Abraham to do something by faith, He was, in essence, entering into a covenant with Abraham. When two people entered into a covenant with one another, there were certain agreements that had to be made, certain promises that were offered and kept. Once you entered into a covenant with someone, it meant that if you expected them to do something for you, then you must be willing to do the same for them.

By entering into a covenant with Abraham, God was saying, "Abraham, I want you to give Me your only son, so that in return, I will then give up My only Son for the sake of the world." He made promises to Abraham that He intended to keep. The one thing He needed from Abraham was faith. When Abraham believed that God would provide a sacrifice—a lamb—to take Isaac's place, God was able to provide that lamb—the Lamb of God, Jesus. In the same way that Abraham had offered up his only son, God the Father offered up His only Son, whose death, burial, and resurrection birthed a new race of spiritual people—the Church of God.

Because Abraham believed God for a son when he was past childbearing age, and because he trusted God to give Isaac back to him from the dead if need be to keep the promise of blessing the world through him, a new race was born. Isaac gave birth to Jacob, who brought forth the twelve sons who became the twelve tribes of Israel.

Galatians 3:27–29

For as many of you as have been baptized into Christ have put on Christ.

There is neither Jew nor Greek, there is neither bond nor free, there is neither male nor female: for ye are all one in Christ Jesus.

And if ye be Christ's, then are ye Abraham's seed, and heirs according to the promise.

From this passage, we see by faith, we who believe in Christ belong to Christ. Just as Abraham believed that God could raise Isaac from the dead in order to keep His promise to Abraham, the same quality of faith is required for us to believe that God raised Jesus from the dead. That's why when we believe in Christ, we become children of Abraham; we have that same spirit of faith. We believe in the God of the resurrection!

And because we belong to Christ, we are the seed of Abraham, and we have inherited the promise God gave to Abraham—the promise to bless the Earth through His seed—Jesus, and His Body, the Church.

IN MY NAME

Romans 4:23–24

Now it was not written for his sake alone, that it was imputed to him;

But for us also, to whom it shall be imputed, if we believe on Him that raised up Jesus our Lord from the dead.

The Bible says that God counted Abraham's faith as righteousness. He saw Abraham as cleansed of sin, through Jesus, even though Jesus was yet to come in the flesh. And God considered Abraham righteous not just for his sake, but for the sake of all of us who would follow in his footsteps and believe in the promises of God. Through us, all the nations of the Earth are blessed, because through us, Christ is present, the power of God is present, and God's will can be done on the Earth. This is the importance of our receiving, trusting in, and walking in the authority Christ won for us on the Cross.

CHAPTER 5

SON OF ADAM — SON OF GOD

Because of the disobedience and rebellion of Adam and Eve, all of humanity became enslaved to sin. In the book of Romans, the full extent of humanity's slavery can be seen. Romans 3 declares that all of us are guilty of sin.

> **Romans 3:10–12**
>
> *As it is written, There is none righteous, no, not one:*
>
> *There is none that understandeth, there is none that seeketh after God.*
>
> *They are all gone out of the way, they are together become unprofitable; there is none that doeth good, no, not one.*

Romans 5:12 follows up on this concept by telling us that Adam's sin in the Garden of Eden is the reason that sin reigns over all mankind—*By one man sin entered into the world, and death by sin*. The story changes in Romans 6 because Paul explains that Christians are no longer slaves to sin, but to righteousness through faith in the finished work of Jesus Christ on the Cross. That freedom and righteousness are what give Christians authority over the devil. (We'll talk about this more in later chapters.)

Right now, though, let's stay focused on what our enslavement to sin was like before Jesus came—so that we can see clearly *why* we need to learn how to exercise our God-given authority in today's world.

Remember, God's original plan was that human beings would rule over His creation. God created the Earth and gave Adam dominion over it. Adam surrendered his dominion by obeying Satan rather than God. This transfer of authority made Satan the god of this world, the prince of the power of the air, while man became slave to sin. Despite Adam's failure, though, God promised to send a Deliverer, and that Deliverer would be the Seed of a Woman.

Remember, also, that everyone born from the time of Adam to this very day has been born a sinner. That condition of sin is now in our spiritual DNA. The Deliverer would have to be a sinless man in order to challenge Satan and take back man's authority. But in order for a man to come into the world sinless, he could not be born through the seed of a natural human father, because the sin nature would be transferred through that seed.

This is why, from the beginning, God promised that *He* would send a coming Deliverer who would deal with Satan and defeat sin once and for all. Human beings, in and of themselves, would not be able to defeat the devil and reclaim authority over the world. Only God could bring such a miracle about.

The Coming Deliverer

From Genesis to Revelation, God tells about the coming Messiah, the Deliverer, the Savior. Moses prophesied, "God will send another prophet like me" (Deuteronomy 18:15; Acts 3:22). Abraham prophesied, "It will be seen in the mountain of the Lord that God Himself will provide a lamb" (Genesis 22:8). David, Isaiah, Jeremiah, and other men of God—they all prophesied about the Coming One.

Satan also knew about the Coming One because of what God said in the Garden of Eden.

> **Genesis 3:15**
> *And I will put enmity between thee and the woman, and between thy seed and her seed; it shall bruise thy head, and thou shalt bruise his heel.*

The way that you destroy a serpent forever is to cut off or crush its head. So, this image in Genesis 3 is a sign that God intended to totally destroy the power of the devil through the Seed of the Woman, the Savior, the Coming One. Needless to say, the devil did not want to be crushed. Every time God was getting ready to work in the Earth, Satan tried to stop the plan of God. And to this day, the devil still tries to stop God's plans from coming to pass.

Before Moses was born, for example, the Pharaoh who reigned in Egypt at the time was inspired by the devil to harm the Israelites who lived in Egypt. He was afraid that the children of Israel would multiply, join with Egypt's enemies, and win their freedom. So, he ordered that all male children of the Jewish slaves be killed.

> **Exodus 1:22**
> *And Pharaoh charged all his people, saying, Every son that is born ye shall cast into the river, and every daughter ye shall save alive.*

This was an evil plan inspired by Satan to stop God's plan for the nation of Israel to be formed. But God prevailed! Moses was born anyway; he was even cared for by a member of the Pharaoh's household (Exodus 2:1–10). And Moses eventually became the deliverer of his people.

The same attack against a coming Deliverer happened when Jesus was born. King Herod ordered that all of the babies born in Bethlehem should be killed in an attempt to stop the Messiah from coming, because it was also prophesied that the Messiah would be a king, and Herod did not want to lose his position (Matthew 2:16–18). Jesus escaped this terrible attack, and He went on to live out His purpose as our Savior and Lord.

In both cases, Satan knew a Deliverer for God's people was coming, but he wasn't sure where or when or who it would be. So, he inspired terrible violence in a vain attempt to stop God's plan to crush him from coming to pass.

The Effects of Spiritual Slavery

In Job 9:32–33, Job said there was no one to stand between himself and God in order to plead Job's case and be his representative. In other words, Job recognized that he needed a mediator—someone to stand in the gap for him and help him obtain justice and freedom from the attacks of the enemy. Job 19 is even clearer about who Job was expecting to help him.

> **Job 19:25–27**
> *For I know that my redeemer liveth, and that he shall stand at the latter day upon the Earth:*

And though after my skin worms destroy this body, yet in my flesh shall I see God:

Whom I shall see for myself, and mine eyes shall behold, and not another; though my reins be consumed within me.

This is one of the Old Testament's greatest prophecies of the coming Savior. It is clear that Job was expecting this Savior to come one day. This revelation serves to highlight the problem that humanity was facing ever since the fall of Adam and Eve in the Garden of Eden.

The problem was this: Mankind was awaiting the promised Messiah, who would one day free them. But their status as slaves meant they had no rights in the day-to-day living of their lives.

Throughout history, various cultures have practiced slavery—so we can look at history to show us the suffering and pain that slavery causes for humanity. The Jews were enslaved in Egypt. Various African people have been enslaved by various cultures, including the Muslims, Europeans, and Americans. In many tribal groups around the world, slavery was a common practice during war. The stronger tribe would conquer the weaker tribe and make that tribe their slaves. These conquered slaves had no legal rights. They were each treated like a piece of property and were not even regarded as people.

Slavery is demeaning. It robs people of their ability to make choices for themselves. It limits people from achieving their full, God-given potential. Slaves are trapped and forced to live according to the whims and will of their master, and often, this results in great suffering, pain, and evil.

Satan has always treated mankind as slaves, and he has been a cruel master. Throughout history, mankind has cried out to God in their suffering, calling out for freedom from their slavery, anxiously awaiting the promised Deliverer—just like the children of Israel cried out for a deliverer before Moses came.

This is where Jesus enters the picture. Known as the last Adam (or sometimes the second Adam), He was born of a virgin, and He came to set mankind free.

Born of a Pure Seed

It's important to remember that during His ministry on Earth, Jesus referred to Himself more frequently as the Son of Man than the Son of God. Now, the New Testament was written in Greek, but Jesus spoke Hebrew. So when He called Himself the Son of Man, He was really saying, "I am the Son of Adam."

This is why Paul refers to Jesus as the last Adam. As the last Adam, Jesus came as a perfect man, without sin. And because Jesus was not a slave of Satan, Satan had no authority over Him. Jesus walked in the authority God intended for Adam to have. And Jesus exercised that authority as a man in the Earth. How did this come about? It came about because Jesus was born of God, not of man—just as the first Adam was.

Jesus was the Seed of a Woman, as prophesied in Genesis 3. What does this mean? In Luke 1, the angel Gabriel came to Mary and told her she would have a son without the help of a man.

> Luke 1:30–35
> *And the angel said unto her, Fear not, Mary: for thou hast found favour with God.*

And, behold, thou shalt conceive in thy womb, and bring forth a son, and shalt call His name Jesus.

He shall be great, and shall be called the Son of the Highest: and the Lord God shall give unto Him the throne of His father David:

And He shall reign over the house of Jacob for ever; and of His Kingdom there shall be no end.

Then said Mary unto the angel, How shall this be, seeing I know not a man?

And the angel answered and said unto her, The Holy Ghost shall come upon thee, and the power of the Highest shall overshadow thee: therefore also that holy thing which shall be born of thee shall be called the Son of God.

Mary asked Gabriel how such a thing could happen to her. She was a virgin, betrothed to Joseph, which meant she had never had a sexual relationship with a man. Mary knew it would be wrong to do so outside of marriage, so she wondered what the prophecy could mean. Gabriel told her the baby would be conceived by the Holy Spirit. The seed would come straight from God Himself.

As previously discussed, our spiritual bloodline comes to us from the man—not the woman. This meant that instead of the seed of a man entering Mary's egg, it was the Holy Ghost who fertilized the egg. The spiritual bloodline of Jesus came from God Himself. This seed was pure and free of the sin that tainted every human being since Adam. This is why only Jesus' blood could pay the price for our sin, as seen in John chapter 1.

John 1:1, 14
In the beginning was the Word, and the Word was with God, and the Word was God.

And the Word was made flesh, and dwelt among us, (and we beheld His glory, the glory as of the only begotten of the Father,) full of grace and truth.

These Scriptures and many others clearly tell us that Jesus would become a man, would die for our sins, and would be raised up by God the Father to a place of authority over the power of Satan. Philippians chapter 2, in particular, points out how Jesus was God, yet He agreed to lay aside His divinity to become a man.

Philippians 2:5–11

Let this mind be in you, which was also in Christ Jesus:

Who, being in the form of God, thought it not robbery to be equal with God:

But made Himself of no reputation, and took upon Him the form of a servant, and was made in the likeness of men:

And being found in fashion as a man, He humbled Himself, and became obedient unto death, even the death of the Cross.

Wherefore God also hath highly exalted Him, and given Him a Name which is above every name:

That at the Name of Jesus every knee should bow, of things in heaven, and things in Earth, and things under the Earth;

And that every tongue should confess that Jesus Christ is Lord, to the glory of God the Father.

It is because Jesus agreed to lay aside His divine nature for a time, coming to Earth in the form of a sinless man, that mankind can walk free of our enslavement to the devil and exercise authority in the Earth.

Fulfilling the Law of Moses

We know that Adam and Eve plunged the human race into sin. We know that Jesus, the Seed of Woman, would one day come and set us free from sin. In the meantime, how was God going to get people to come to Him? How was He going to save people? Keep in mind that everyone was a slave to sin before Jesus made a way.

> **Galatians 4:4–5**
> *But when the fulness of the time was come, God sent forth His Son, made of a woman, made under the Law,*
>
> *To redeem them that were under the law, that we might receive the adoption of sons.*

Paul explains to us in Galatians that the Law was given until the time that Jesus would come. The Law of Moses was a picture of God's perfect standards, the essence of His holiness and perfection. Of course, none of us can meet the high standards of the Law, which is another reason the Law was given: to expose sin.

> **Romans 3:20**
> *Therefore by the deeds of the Law there shall no flesh be justified in his sight: for by the Law is the knowledge of sin.*

> **Galatians 3:11**
> *But that no man is justified by the Law in the sight of God, it is evident: for, The just shall live by faith.*

God knew human beings would not be able to keep the Law of Moses. They would need a way to be made for the forgiveness of their transgressions against the Law. So, when God gave the Law, He also instituted sacrifices. The purpose of the sacrifices was to make a way—through the blood of innocent, perfect animals—for man to atone for their sin. These animal sacrifices were a temporary solution for their sin problem, but because the sacrifices were being faithfully made, it allowed the children of Israel to fellowship with God.

Finally, in the fullness of time, after many centuries of man failing to keep the Law, Jesus came to the Earth. He came as the Seed of Woman, with holy blood, the only blood that could take away the sin of man. Until Jesus was crucified, mankind remained a slave to sin. However, Jesus had authority over the devil, even in His human form, because He was sinless. His authority can be seen in John 14:30.

> **John 14:30b**
> *...the prince of this world cometh, and hath nothing in me.*

In this verse, Jesus declared that the prince of the world—Satan—had no authority over Him. The only reason Satan had no authority over the Lord was that Jesus was sinless.

> **John 8:34–36**
> *Jesus answered them, Verily, verily, I say unto you, Whosoever committeth sin is the servant of sin.*
>
> *And the servant abideth not in the house for ever: but the Son abideth ever.*
>
> *If the Son therefore shall make you free, ye shall be free indeed.*

Jesus said that whoever commits sin is a slave to sin. He then said that Satan, the serpent, had no authority over Him. Jesus' follow-up statement once again points to His authority over the devil and His ability to set us free from sin.

Destroying the Works of the Devil

When Jesus came as the last Adam, the Seed of Woman, He came to destroy the works of Satan.

1 John 3:8b
For this purpose the Son of God was manifested, that He might destroy the works of the devil.

What are the works of Satan? Sin, sickness, death, and all kinds of evil. Did Jesus destroy those works at every opportunity? Yes, He did!

Jesus fulfilled the purpose He came to fulfill. He was tempted, just like Adam and Eve were tempted. But He did not fail like Adam, nor did He surrender any authority. When Satan saw Jesus' ministry, he saw a problem. For the first time since Adam, there was a man Satan could not control.

Peter tells us in Acts 10:38 that everywhere Jesus went on the Earth, He destroyed the works of Satan. And Satan was completely powerless to stop Jesus because Satan had no authority in Jesus' life. This was only possible because Jesus was not a slave to sin.

Let's look at Jesus' authority to destroy the works of the devil in more detail. In Luke 4, Jesus was in the synagogue reading from Isaiah. Here's what He said of Himself and His purpose for coming to Earth:

> **Luke 4:18–19**
>
> *The Spirit of the Lord is upon me, because He hath anointed Me to preach the Gospel to the poor; He hath sent Me to heal the brokenhearted, to preach deliverance to the captives, and recovering of sight to the blind, to set at liberty them that are bruised,*
>
> *To preach the acceptable year of the Lord.*

Everywhere Jesus went, He preached the Word of God. He forgave sins, healed sicknesses and diseases, cast out devils, and preached the Kingdom of God. He was constantly doing good and setting free those who were oppressed by the devil. Satan could not stop Him. Even the religious leaders could not stop Him because Jesus, as the Son of Man, had authority. Jesus came to destroy the works of Satan—and He fulfilled that purpose daily during His earthly ministry.

And He still does so, through us, the Church!

The Authority of Jesus During His Ministry

> **Romans 6:16–18**
>
> *Know ye not, that to whom ye yield yourselves servants to obey, his servants ye are to whom ye obey; whether of sin unto death, or of obedience unto righteousness?*
>
> *But God be thanked, that ye were the servants of sin, but ye have obeyed from the heart that form of doctrine which was delivered you.*
>
> *Being then made free from sin, ye became the servants of righteousness.*

As we have already discussed, the Deliverer who would free humanity from spiritual slavery had to be a sinless man. And Jesus indeed came as a sinless man—born of God through a virgin named Mary—to restore man's authority. But did Jesus truly have authority in the Earth—the authority over the devil and over creation that God intended the first Adam to have in the Book of Genesis?

Yes, He did. Jesus walked in the full authority God intended human beings to have and enjoy. How do we know this to be true?

One passage that points to the nature and extent of Jesus' authority in the Earth can be found in Matthew 21.

> **Matthew 21:23–27**
>
> *And when He was come into the temple, the chief priests and the elders of the people came unto Him as He was teaching, and said, By what authority doest thou these things? and who gave Thee this authority?*
>
> *And Jesus answered and said unto them, I also will ask you one thing, which if ye tell Me, I in like wise will tell you by what authority I do these things.*
>
> *The baptism of John, whence was it? from heaven, or of men? And they reasoned with themselves, saying, If we shall say, From heaven; He will say unto us, Why did ye not then believe him?*
>
> *But if we shall say, Of men; we fear the people; for all hold John as a prophet.*
>
> *And they answered Jesus, and said, We cannot tell. And He said unto them, Neither tell I you by what authority I do these things.*

We see in this passage that the Pharisees came to Jesus with a question: "By what authority do You do what You do?" They were referring to the miracles He was performing—the healings, the deliverances, the preaching of the Word of God, the forgiveness of sinners. The Pharisees hoped, as always, to catch Jesus saying something blasphemous so that they could condemn Him and discredit His ministry. So, they dared Him to make a statement about where the miracle-working power was coming from.

Rather than making a statement, Jesus answered their question with a question of His own: "Who gave John the Baptist his authority—God or men?" Jesus' question led to an argument amongst the Pharisees.

If they claimed that John the Baptist got his authority from man, they would be implying that John was a false prophet. The crowds would riot at that statement, because they believed John was a true prophet. However, if the Pharisees said his authority came from God, then Jesus would ask the leaders why they refused to believe John the Baptist when he declared that Jesus was *the Lamb of God, which taketh away the sin of the world* (John 1:29).

Unsure of what to do, trapped by the question, the Pharisees replied, "We don't know."

Jesus said, "Then I'm not going to tell you where I get My authority." He refused to be trapped by them. And He didn't need to defend Himself, because the miracles He was doing were proof, in themselves, that He had authority in the Earth.

John 10:37–38
If I do not the works of My Father, believe Me not.

But if I do, though ye believe not Me, believe the works: that ye may know, and believe, that the Father is in Me, and I in Him.

In this passage, Jesus told the Pharisees that even if they did not want to believe His words, they should at least look at the evidence of His power in the Earth to know that God had sent Him. The works Jesus did were proof of the authority He had over the devil.

Authority to Forgive and to Heal

In Luke 5, the story of the lame man and his four friends is an example of Jesus' authority.

> **Luke 5:17–26**
>
> *And it came to pass on a certain day, as He was teaching, that there were Pharisees and doctors of the Law sitting by, which were come out of every town of Galilee, and Judaea, and Jerusalem: and the power of the Lord was present to heal them.*
>
> *And, behold, men brought in a bed a man which was taken with a palsy: and they sought means to bring him in, and to lay him before Him.*
>
> *And when they could not find by what way they might bring him in because of the multitude, they went upon the housetop, and let him down through the tiling with his couch into the midst before Jesus.*
>
> *And when He saw their faith, He said unto him, Man, thy sins are forgiven thee.*
>
> *And the scribes and the Pharisees began to reason, saying, Who is this which speaketh blasphemies? Who can forgive sins, but God alone?*
>
> *But when Jesus perceived their thoughts, He answering said unto them, What reason ye in your hearts?*
>
> *Whether is easier, to say, Thy sins be forgiven thee; or to say, Rise up and walk?*
>
> *But that ye may know that the Son of man hath power upon Earth to forgive sins, (He said unto the sick of the palsy,) I say unto thee, Arise, and take up thy couch, and go*

into thine house.

And immediately he rose up before them, and took up that whereon he lay, and departed to his own house, glorifying God.

And they were all amazed, and they glorified God, and were filled with fear, saying, We have seen strange things to day.

Four friends brought their friend to Jesus because he was lame. When the friends saw that the house was full, they climbed up on the roof and then lowered their friend down to Jesus as He was teaching. Jesus saw the man coming, and seeing the faith of the friends, He said to the lame man, "Your sins are forgiven."

The religious leaders became upset because of Jesus' answer. They said, "Who does this man think He is that He can forgive sins? Only God can forgive sins!"

Jesus answered, "What is easier to say: your sins are forgiven, or rise, take up your bed, and walk?" Then, so that they would know He had authority on the Earth to forgive sins as well as to heal, He said to the man, "Rise, pick up your bed, and go to your house." And the man rose up, healed.

This account of the man's healing is interesting in terms of what it shows us about the power of God and the authority that He intended mankind to exercise over creation. It is clear from the passage that Jesus viewed the man's forgiveness as equal to his healing. Both were valuable. Both were solutions to the suffering that results from sin and the enslavement of humanity by the devil. Both were evidence of God's plan for man—His best wishes for us.

Jesus said, "What's easier to say: you're forgiven, or rise up and walk?" This meant, "Which is easier to accomplish: forgiveness from sin or healing from a physical ailment that doesn't heal on its own?" Both are equally impossible for man to bring about. Both are possible only through God's intervention. And both are inextricably linked by what Jesus would accomplish through His death, resurrection, and ascension.

Notice the answer Jesus gave in verse 24: *But that ye may know that the Son of man hath power upon Earth to forgive sins, (He said unto the sick of the palsy,) I say unto thee, Arise, and take up thy couch, and go into thine house.* The healing power of God at work through Jesus was evidence that He had power over sin as well.

We see this evidence again when John the Baptist was arrested. As the forerunner to Jesus, John the Baptist preached repentance, baptized people, and prepared the way for Jesus to begin His ministry. Later on, however, John the Baptist was arrested and thrown in prison. When he was sentenced to death, John began to struggle with doubt.

> **Luke 7:19**
> *And John calling unto him two of his disciples sent them to Jesus, saying, Art thou he that should come? or look we for another?*

John the Baptist wanted to make sure he was dying for the truth. So, he asked Jesus, "Are You the One we've been waiting for? Or do we need to look for someone else?" What did Jesus give as evidence of His identity?

> **Luke 7:21–22**
> *And in that same hour He cured many of their infirmities and plagues, and of evil spirits; and unto many that were blind He gave sight.*

> *Then Jesus answering said unto them, Go your way, and tell John what things ye have seen and heard; how that the blind see, the lame walk, the lepers are cleansed, the deaf hear, the dead are raised, to the poor the Gospel is preached.*

The proof that Jesus was the Messiah, the promised Deliverer, was His power over the devil. Jesus was destroying the works of Satan. Throughout His earthly ministry, He had authority over Satan, which He proved every time He performed a miracle, sign, or wonder. Jesus was even able to delegate authority to His disciples. Several times, Jesus sent the disciples out with instructions to heal the sick and cast out devils.

In Luke 10, Jesus sent out seventy disciples with instructions to heal the sick and cast out devils.

> **Luke 10:9, 17–19**
>
> *...heal the sick that are therein, and say unto them, The kingdom of God is come nigh unto you.*
>
> *And the seventy returned again with joy, saying, Lord, even the devils are subject unto us through Thy name.*
>
> *And He said unto them, I beheld Satan as lightning fall from heaven.*
>
> *Behold, I give unto you power to tread on serpents and scorpions, and over all the power of the enemy: and nothing shall by any means hurt you.*

While Jesus was on the Earth, He not only had authority over the devil; He was also able to give, or delegate, that authority to His disciples by instructing them to use His Name, in faith.

Authority Even to Control When His Time Had Come

Satan was stopped in his tracks because he could not stop Jesus. Time after time, the religious leaders tried to kill or trap Jesus, but they could not. Both the devil and the people he worked through to cause trouble could not stop Jesus—until Jesus Himself, and God the Father, were ready for Jesus to die on the Cross. Jesus referred to His prophesied death as His hour or time coming, and it is clear that even in that arena, He had authority over the devil.

In John 2:4, Jesus' first miracle is recorded. During a wedding feast, his mother, Mary, came to Jesus because the wine had run out. Jesus' answer is interesting:

John 2:4
Jesus saith unto her, Woman, what have I to do with thee? Mine hour is not yet come.

Mary wanted Jesus to do something, but He said, "My hour has not yet come." Then He told the servants what to do. The miracle took place, but Jesus, from the very start of His ministry, declared when His time would come—and when it had not yet come. Jesus' death would not happen according to the devil's timing, but according to God's perfect timing.

In both John 7:30 and John 8:20, the religious leaders wanted to kill Jesus, but they could not do so, because His hour had not yet come. All throughout Jesus' life and ministry, Satan could not touch Him.

John 10:17–18
Therefore doth My Father love Me, because I lay down My life, that I might take it again.

> *No man taketh it from Me, but I lay it down of myself. I have power to lay it down, and I have power to take it again. This commandment have I received of My Father.*

Here, Jesus makes it clear that His authority is so potent, not even Satan could kill Him until His hour had come. Even when it was time for Jesus to die, Jesus had to willingly drop His protection.

When the soldiers came to arrest Jesus in the Garden of Gethsemane, they came with swords and clubs. However, one word from Jesus—"I am," to be exact—made them all fall to the ground. This event was meant to demonstrate that Jesus was still in control.

Peter didn't understand that Jesus had authority even over the timing of His death. So, Peter responded in a human, natural fashion—he tried to protect Jesus by cutting off one of the guard's ears with His sword. Notice how Jesus responded.

> **Matthew 26:53–54**
>
> *Thinkest thou that I cannot now pray to My Father, and He shall presently give Me more than twelve legions of angels?*
>
> *But how then shall the scriptures be fulfilled, that thus it must be?*

Jesus chastised Peter and then told him twelve legions of angels could come down to save Jesus if He wanted any help. Satan could not kill Jesus if Jesus didn't allow it. The Lord was choosing to allow Himself to be arrested, tried, and executed on the Cross so that the prophecy of a Deliverer who would set mankind free from sin would be fulfilled.

Jesus Maintained His Authority, Even at His Crucifixion

All throughout His life and ministry, Jesus declared, "My hour has not yet come." But when the time for God's plan to free us of sin had fully arrived, Jesus began to talk about dying and giving His life for us.

> **John 12:23–27**
>
> *And Jesus answered them, saying, The hour is come, that the Son of man should be glorified.*
>
> *Verily, verily, I say unto you, Except a corn of wheat fall into the ground and die, it abideth alone: but if it die, it bringeth forth much fruit.*
>
> *He that loveth his life shall lose it; and he that hateth his life in this world shall keep it unto life eternal.*
>
> *If any man serve Me, let him follow Me; and where I am, there shall also My servant be: if any man serve Me, him will My Father honour.*
>
> *Now is My soul troubled; and what shall I say? Father, save Me from this hour: but for this cause came I unto this hour.*

At last, Jesus' hour had come—and Satan, the prince of the world, would be cast out. This is the fulfillment of Genesis 3:15. The seed of the serpent would bruise the Seed of the Woman's heel, but He would crush the serpent's head. The devil sensed that he was in danger, so he looked for a way of escape. He found what he thought was an opportunity through Judas.

> **John 13:21, 26–27**
>
> *When Jesus had thus said, he was troubled in spirit, and testified, and said, Verily, verily,*

> *I say unto you, that one of you shall betray Me.*
>
> *Jesus answered, He it is, to whom I shall give a sop, when I have dipped it. And when He had dipped the sop, He gave it to Judas Iscariot, the son of Simon.*
>
> *And after the sop Satan entered into him. Then said Jesus unto him, That thou doest, do quickly.*

Satan believed he'd found an opening to come against Jesus through Judas' betrayal. Satan was thinking, "I'm going to destroy Jesus!" However, God had a bigger plan behind the crucifixion.

> **John 12:28b, 30–32**
>
> *Then came there a voice from heaven, saying, I have both glorified it, and will glorify it again.*
>
> *Jesus answered and said, This voice came not because of Me, but for your sakes.*
>
> *Now is the judgment of this world: now shall the prince of this world be cast out.*
>
> *And I, if I be lifted up from the Earth, will draw all men unto Me.*

All the suffering Jesus would face on the Cross was part of the plan of God. All throughout the Gospel of John, Jesus was telling the disciples about God's plan, but the disciples didn't understand. And in the middle of explaining the plan, Jesus told the disciples about the coming of the Holy Spirit, who would help them understand everything.

No one understood the plan of God. Not man. Not devils. Not even the angels, though they wanted to understand, because they knew something major was about to happen. The Seed of the Woman was about to crush the head of the serpent. Satan, however, thought he had finally found a way to destroy Jesus.

What Satan didn't know was that God was working His own plan. As Jesus was walking with His disciples from the upper room to the garden, He stopped to offer up a prayer.

John 17:1–5

These words spake Jesus, and lifted up His eyes to heaven, and said, Father, the hour is come; glorify Thy Son, that Thy Son also may glorify Thee:

As Thou hast given Him power over all flesh, that He should give eternal life to as many as Thou hast given Him.

And this is life eternal, that they might know Thee the only true God, and Jesus Christ, whom Thou hast sent.

I have glorified Thee on the Earth: I have finished the work which Thou gavest Me to do.

And now, O Father, glorify Thou Me with Thine own self with the glory which I had with Thee before the world was.

In these passages, as Jesus is speaking to His disciples prior to His coming death on the Cross, we learn two important things. First, we learn that God's plan involves the judgment of the devil. Satan will be cast out, and mankind will be drawn to Jesus and freed from their sin through faith in Him. Second, now that it is time for Jesus to die on the Cross, He will be returning to His position in Heaven at God's right hand. He will be glorified.

The Mystery of God's Plan

> **1 Corinthians 2:7–8**
> *But we speak the wisdom of God in a mystery, even the hidden wisdom, which God ordained before the world unto our glory:*
>
> *Which none of the princes of this world knew: for had they known it, they would not have crucified the Lord of glory.*

There was a mystery that Satan didn't understand about Jesus. God kept His plan for delivering mankind from their slavery to sin and death, and His plan to take back man's lost authority, a secret so that Satan wouldn't know what was happening and would not be able to interfere. While Satan acted, thinking he was destroying Jesus, he was actually being led into a trap that would guarantee his own destruction. This is what happened when Satan had Jesus crucified. Satan's plan was foiled because Jesus was not a slave to sin.

In countries where slavery was practiced, killing a slave was not considered murder because a slave was considered a piece of property. However, if a man killed his neighbor, that man would be guilty of murder. One of the things that happened when Satan killed Jesus was that Satan had overstepped his authority. Jesus was not his slave, yet he killed Him. Through this act, Satan became a murderer, condemning himself, because he killed an innocent man.

> **John 8:44b**
> *...He was a murderer from the beginning, and abode not in the truth, because there is no truth in him. When he speaketh a lie, he speaketh of his own: for he is a liar, and the father of it.*

Satan has always been a murderer, wreaking death and destruction on the human race. Yet technically, they were all his slaves. While we know that Satan was full of hatred from the beginning, it wasn't until Jesus was crucified that Satan actually committed an act of murder by putting to death Someone that he had no authority over. Jesus is called the Lamb that was slain before the foundation of Earth, because it was always God's plan that Jesus would die in our place, and thus pay the price for our sin, setting us free. And while Jesus was called the Lamb that was slain before the foundation of the world, it wasn't until He was crucified that He became the Lamb of God.

Satan was condemned in the courts of Heaven as a murderer the moment he had Jesus crucified. He shed Jesus' innocent blood. That was the moment that everything was turned around. Satan was defeated, and mankind was set free from slavery to him. Satan brought the condemnation on himself, and the fulfillment of Genesis 3 was complete—the serpent would bruise Jesus' heel, but Jesus' heel would crush the devil's head.

SECTION 2:

The Scriptural Restoration of the Believer's Authority

CHAPTER 6

CRUCIFIXION, DEATH, BURIAL, RESURRECTION AND ASCENSION

When Jesus gave His life for us on the Cross, the victory of God was complete and wonderful. There is now no reason for us to fear Satan ever again! What does this victory look like? And how do we see it through what Jesus did for us? Let's take a look at what the Bible tells us.

The Lamb of God—the Perfect Sacrifice

In the Bible, whenever God makes a covenant with mankind, a sacrifice is offered, often a sacrifice of a slain animal. This shedding of blood would temporarily cover the sins of the people who were approaching God. But these sacrifices were just a foreshadowing of what was to come in Christ—the perfect sacrifice.

> **1 Peter 1:19–20**
> *But with the precious blood of Christ, as of a lamb without blemish and without spot:*
>
> *Who verily was foreordained before the foundation of the world, but was manifest in these last times for you.*

Jesus is the Lamb of God, the perfect sacrifice to set us free from the power of sin and death, and from our enslavement to the devil. How is this possible? It is through His blood that we are cleansed and freed. Like a lamb without blemish, Jesus was sinless. And His sinlessness qualified Him to be a sacrifice to pay the price for mankind's sins.

> **1 John 1:7**
> *But if we walk in the light, as He is in the light, we have fellowship one with another, and the blood of Jesus Christ His Son cleanseth us from all sin.*

Because Jesus is both sinless and the Son of God, His blood is the only blood that can wash away sin. And it does so perfectly. When we are born again, His blood cleanses us completely.

> **Revelation 5:12**
> *Saying with a loud voice, Worthy is the Lamb that was slain to receive power, and riches, and wisdom, and strength, and honour, and glory, and blessing.*

Jesus, as a sinless man and the Son of God, was, is, and always will be worthy to be seated at the right hand of God—which is where we are also seated, as part of His Body.

No More Condemnation

> **Colossians 2:13–15**
> *And you, being dead in your sins and the uncircumcision of your flesh, hath he quickened together with him, having forgiven you all trespasses;*

CRUCIFIXION, DEATH, BURIAL, RESURRECTION AND ASCENSION

Blotting out the handwriting of ordinances that was against us, which was contrary to us, and took it out of the way, nailing it to His Cross;

And having spoiled principalities and powers, He made a shew of them openly, triumphing over them in it.

Jesus spoiled principalities and powers, triumphing over them through the Cross, and enabling us to reign with Him in life. How did He spoil the devil? Through the Cross, Jesus blotted out the handwriting of ordinances that was against us, and He nailed it to the Cross.

What does the Scripture mean when it talks about *the handwriting of ordinances that was against us*? The word *ordinance* refers to a governmental law, specifically a law set forth by God. So, the word *ordinances* in this verse refers to the laws of God set forth in the Old Testament, especially in the Law of Moses—everything God has said, everything that defines what God desires of His people, what He considers obedience, and what He considers sin.

The *handwriting* of these ordinances refers to the judgment made against us because we broke God's Law. Because we were all guilty of breaking God's Law, the curse and condemnation of the Law belonged to us, according to Deuteronomy 28. Therefore, we were all subject to the curse of the Law. The ultimate result of that curse is spiritual death—separation from God for all eternity. Because all have sinned and fallen short of the glory of God, we all have received a judgment against us that says GUILTY.

Jesus came to Earth to do something about this guilty verdict against mankind. And in Colossians 2:13–15, it is made clear how Jesus addressed our guilty verdict. Verse 14 says He took the handwriting that was against us, the sentence of death we deserved as a result of our sin, and nailed it to His Cross.

We owed a price—death, and separation from God. But Jesus paid that price on our behalf. And because He paid the price for our sins, there are no longer any legal grounds for the curse to be enacted in our lives. Satan has no legal right to oppress us any longer, because Jesus paid the price for our sins and then stripped the devil of the authority he had over us.

I have a nephew who retired after many years on his local police force. During his work hours, he would deal with criminals as lawbreakers, and submit them to the consequences of the law. He had two sons at home during that time. Now, if he came home from work and found he had to discipline them for being disobedient, he did not arrest them and take them down to jail for breaking the law. He disciplined them as their father in order for them to learn obedience. So it is with us and our Heavenly Father.

Christians are not under the condemnation of the Law anymore! Even though we can still make mistakes after we are born again, we are not treated as lawbreakers deserving of death, because Christ's blood cleanses us.

Free from the Curse of the Law

Galatians 3:13–14

Christ hath redeemed us from the curse of the Law, being made a curse for us: for it is written, Cursed is every one that hangeth on a tree:

That the blessing of Abraham might come on the Gentiles through Jesus Christ; that we might receive the promise of the Spirit through faith.

CRUCIFIXION, DEATH, BURIAL, RESURRECTION AND ASCENSION

Jesus became a curse for us on the Cross, so that the blessing God promised to Abraham and his descendants would come upon us as well. And by faith, we can receive the benefits of what He did for us—in every area of our lives. The moment we realize Satan is defeated, that Jesus has already provided healing and forgiveness, our lives will be forever changed.

2 Corinthians 5:21
For He hath made Him to be sin for us, who knew no sin; that we might be made the righteousness of God in Him.

Jesus made us righteous in His sight through His death and resurrection. We are no longer guilty of sin in His eyes. We no longer bear the curse that comes from sin and death. What does this mean?

Remember, God gave the Ten Commandments and the Law of Moses as an example of His standard of perfection. No one could live up to the Law or fulfill it. None of us could fully obey the Law, because all of us sin and fall short of God's glory (Romans 3:23). This is why God the Father sent Jesus.

Romans 8:3
For what the Law could not do, in that it was weak through the flesh, God sending His own Son in the likeness of sinful flesh, and for sin, condemned sin in the flesh.

The Law could never make anybody perfect or righteous in God's eyes, because no one could live up to the standard of the Law. Our flesh, our sinful nature, hinders our obedience to God. As a result, human beings have always ended up breaking some portion of the Law.

And the Bible says that those who break any portion of the Law are guilty of all of it (James 2:10).

A good example to illustrate our inadequacy to obey the Law is a chain. No matter how strong the chain, it can only be as strong as the weakest link of the chain. The Law was the chain and we, sinful man, were the weak link. This is why the Law could not make us righteous.

To deal with sin once and for all, God sent Jesus in the likeness of human flesh. And by His death on the Cross, Jesus condemned sin in His flesh.

> **Matthew 5:17**
> *...I did not come to destroy the Law… but to fulfill it.*

Jesus, as the last Adam, said, "I didn't come to destroy the Law, but to fulfill it." How did Jesus fulfill the Law? He lived as a sinless man and obeyed the Law completely, in every way, all the way to the Cross. Jesus did what we could not do. He fulfilled all of the requirements of the Law in our place, because we were unable to do it ourselves.

He lived a perfect life, and then on the Cross, He took on all the punishments we deserved through our sinfulness. Jesus became sickness. Jesus became sin. Jesus became cursed. And He took the punishment that we all rightfully deserved. Jesus' life and death fulfilled the Law.

One of the last things Jesus said on the Cross was, "It is finished"—meaning that Jesus fulfilled it all—the blessings and the curses of the Law. He nailed it all to His Cross and said, "It's been paid in full."

What is the curse of the Law? We find the answer in Deuteronomy chapter 28. The first 14 verses of this chapter show us the blessings of obeying the Law, but the rest of the chapter tells of the curses of the Law that will come upon those who do not obey it.

> **Deuteronomy 28:15**
> *But it shall come to pass, if thou wilt not hearken unto the voice of the Lord thy God, to observe to do all His commandments and His statutes which I command thee this day; that all these curses shall come upon thee, and overtake thee.*

The curse of the Law was essentially a list of all the things humanity has suffered because we were made slaves to Satan since Adam fell. Among the many curses the chapter lists are pestilence, fever, consumption, crop failure, bone and joint problems, the kidnapping of children by pagans, marriage problems, and many other griefs. In case anything was left out, Deuteronomy 28:61 has it covered.

> **Deuteronomy 28:61**
> *Also every sickness, and every plague, which is not written in the book of this Law, them will the Lord bring upon thee, until thou be destroyed.*

Even if something is not specifically listed in Deuteronomy 28, if it is evil, if it causes suffering, then it is part of the curse. This was our heritage through the sin of Adam. But Jesus freed us from it all!

We Are Healed Through the Cross

Now, in Isaiah 53, let's look a little more closely at the healing that is ours because Jesus gave His life for us on the Cross.

> **Isaiah 53:4–6**
>
> *Surely He hath borne our griefs, and carried our sorrows: yet we did esteem Him stricken, smitten of God, and afflicted.*
>
> *But He was wounded for our transgressions, He was bruised for our iniquities: the chastisement of our peace was upon Him; and with His stripes we are healed.*
>
> *All we like sheep have gone astray; we have turned every one to his own way; and the Lord hath laid on Him the iniquity of us all.*

On the Cross, Jesus was made sickness as well as sin for us. This was something that He willingly did, which is why no one could touch Him until His hour had come. Jesus allowed Himself to become the Lamb of God sacrificed for our sins.

> **Isaiah 53:10–11**
>
> *Yet it pleased the Lord to bruise Him; He hath put Him to grief: when Thou shalt make His soul an offering for sin, He shall see His seed, He shall prolong His days, and the pleasure of the Lord shall prosper in His hand.*
>
> *He shall see of the travail of His soul, and shall be satisfied: by His knowledge shall My righteous servant justify many; for He shall bear their iniquities.*

Isaiah 53:10 tells us that it pleased the Lord to bruise Jesus, to cause Him pain and make Him sick. You won't see this concept in most modern translations of the Bible, but this is actually what the Scripture says in the original Hebrew language in which the book of Isaiah was written. The same word used to describe our sickness in verse 4 is used in verse 10 where it says the Lord was pleased to put our sickness upon Jesus, making Him carry it on our behalf on the Cross.

Isaiah 53:11 is talking about Jesus as well. Through His knowledge, the Righteous One, Jesus, will make many people righteous. On the Cross, Jesus became sickness and sin so that many, through His knowledge, would be made righteous. As we know Him and receive Him as Lord and Savior, we are forgiven and made righteous in the eyes of God. And Isaiah 53:5 says that by Jesus' wounds or stripes, we are healed.

We Are Made Righteous Through Faith

Galatians 3:13
Christ hath redeemed us from the curse of the Law, being made a curse for us: for it is written, Cursed is every one that hangeth on a tree.

In His life on Earth as the Son of Adam, Jesus fulfilled the Law. In His death, Jesus took upon Himself the curse of the Law and the judgment we all deserved. All of the demands of the Law were met by Jesus. Therefore, anyone who puts their faith in Him receives His righteousness. When we were imperfect and sinful, unable to obey the Law, Jesus did it all for us! As we put our faith in Jesus, in the righteousness He earned for us, we become righteous like Him. As the exalted, glorified Son of God, Jesus has made us righteous before God.

Romans 5:1–2
Therefore being justified by faith, we have peace with God through our Lord Jesus Christ:

By whom also we have access by faith into this grace wherein we stand, and rejoice in hope of the glory of God.

Romans 5:8–9

But God commendeth His love toward us, in that, while we were yet sinners, Christ died for us.

Much more then, being now justified by His blood, we shall be saved from wrath through Him.

We have been made righteous by our faith in Jesus. We have peace with God now. God has now forgiven us and accepted us. There is no animosity between God and people. He is not angry at us. He loves us and is willing to receive us. The only thing that remains is for us to accept Him into our lives, as He has accepted us through Christ. As we open our hearts to Him by faith, receiving Him as Lord and Savior, He gladly comes in and makes His home in our hearts.

2 Corinthians 5:21

For He hath made Him to be sin for us, who knew no sin; that we might be made the righteousness of God in Him.

Jesus became sin so that you and I would be righteous in God's eyes. This right standing and peace with God are essential to walking in our authority. It is because we are righteous in His eyes that we can ask and then expect to receive what we ask for (John 15:7).

And we already know from Galatians that Jesus became cursed so that you and I would be blessed.

Romans 5:17

For if by one man's offence death reigned by one; much more they which receive abun-

dance of grace and of the gift of righteousness shall reign in life by one, Jesus Christ.

1 Peter 2:24
Who His own self bare our sins in His own body on the tree, that we, being dead to sins, should live unto righteousness: by whose stripes ye were healed.

Part of the blessing of God is the renewed ability to walk in His authority in the Earth, to reign in life as kings. Another portion of the blessing is healing. All of these blessings were obtained for us through the finished work of the Cross.

Righteousness Verified by Resurrection

Our salvation, though purchased at the Cross, depended on Jesus being raised from the dead to verify it and establish our righteousness.

Romans 4:25
Who was delivered for our offences, and was raised again for our justification.

This verse tells us He was put to death for our sins—to pay the debt we owed—and this act provided for our forgiveness. However, just being forgiven was not enough. He had to change our nature and make us righteous. This part of the work was accomplished in His Resurrection. Remember our scripture in Ephesians 1 where Paul prayed that believers would understand the exceeding greatness of His power to us who believe—and then he compared it to what happened when Jesus was raised from the dead!

The early disciples knew the importance of the Resurrection. They preached it and were persecuted for it (Acts 4:2). They demonstrated it by signs and wonders:

> **Acts 4:33**
> *And with great power gave the apostles witness of the resurrection of the Lord Jesus: and great grace was upon them all.*

Peter tells us that it is the Resurrection that caused us to be born again.

> **1 Peter 1:3**
> *Blessed be the God and Father of our Lord Jesus Christ, which according to His abundant mercy hath begotten us again unto a lively hope by the resurrection of Jesus Christ from the dead.*

And Paul tells us how to be saved: by believing God has raised Jesus from the dead.

> **Romans 10:9–10**
> *That if thou shalt confess with thy mouth the Lord Jesus, and shalt believe in thine heart that God hath raised him from the dead, thou shalt be saved.*
>
> *For with the heart man believeth unto righteousness; and with the mouth confession is made unto salvation.*

It's not enough to believe Jesus died on the Cross. Even sinners can believe He died. But we must believe He conquered death and rose

CRUCIFIXION, DEATH, BURIAL, RESURRECTION AND ASCENSION

again physically from the dead. This is what makes us "righteous."

> **Romans 4:24–25**
> *But for us also, to whom it [righteousness] shall be imputed, if we believe on him that raised up Jesus our Lord from the dead;*
>
> *Who was delivered for our offences, and was raised again for our justification [righteousness].*

In the Gospel of John, Jesus said one of the works of the Holy Spirit was to convict the world of *"righteousness, because I go to my Father, and ye see me no more"* (John 16:10).

Satan Has Been Stripped of His Power

Everything we've discussed here so far illustrates God's plan for Jesus and the Cross of Calvary. And it was a plan that Satan didn't know anything about until after Jesus did all He came to do. God stripped Satan of his power, and Satan was powerless to prevent it.

Jesus cried out on the Cross, "My God, My God, why have You forsaken Me?" He became forsaken, so we could be forgiven. Why would the Father turn away from Jesus? Because He had become our sin, our sickness, and our curse. This was how God made it possible for us to come back to Him! His righteousness is truly a gift.

> **Romans 5:16–17**
> *And not as it was by one that sinned, so is the gift: for the judgment was by one to condemnation, but the free gift is of many offences unto justification.*

> *For if by one man's offence death reigned by one; much more they which receive abundance of grace and of the gift of righteousness shall reign in life by one, Jesus Christ.*

> **Colossians 2:15**
> *And having spoiled principalities and powers, He made a shew of them openly, triumphing over them in it.*

The righteousness we have through faith in Jesus is directly related to our authority over Satan. It's a gift—not something we can earn. We can only be righteous now because of Jesus. He did what we could not by fulfilling the Law and taking our punishment.

No Longer Condemned

As believers, we are in Christ, and Satan has no more right to rule over our lives. He has no authority any longer to condemn us, because the blood of Jesus has paid the price for us.

But as the accuser of the brethren, he stands before God night and day *trying* to condemn us. He will come before the throne of God, and he will come to us, making accusations. He says, "This sister and brother sinned! Look what they did wrong!"

However, we have overcome him by the blood of the Lamb (Revelation 12:10–11). What does that mean? Simply put, all of Satan's accusations against us mean nothing to God—they have no legal weight—because of the blood of Jesus. This is how we have victory through the Cross. God does not see sin when He looks at us; He sees the shed blood of Jesus that cleanses us of sin.

CRUCIFIXION, DEATH, BURIAL, RESURRECTION AND ASCENSION

Romans 8:1–4 (NKJV)

There is therefore now no condemnation to those who are in Christ Jesus, who do not walk according to the flesh, but according to the Spirit.

For the law of the Spirit of life in Christ Jesus has made me free from the law of sin and death.

For what the law could not do in that it was weak through the flesh, God did by sending His own Son in the likeness of sinful flesh, on account of sin: He condemned sin in the flesh,

That the righteous requirement of the Law might be fulfilled in us who do not walk according to the flesh but according to the Spirit.

When Jesus died on the Cross, He took away the condemnation of the Law, and took away Satan's right to condemn us! When He rose from the dead, He made us righteous!

All Things Are Under His Feet—and Ours

Hebrews 1:1–4 (NKJV)

God, who at various times and in various ways spoke in time past to the fathers by the prophets,

Has in these last days spoken to us by His Son, whom He has appointed heir of all things, through whom also He made the worlds;

Who being the brightness of His glory and the express image of His person, and upholding all things by the word of His power, when He had by Himself purged our sins, sat down at the right hand of the Majesty on high,

> *Having become so much better than the angels, as He has by inheritance obtained a more excellent Name than they.*

When Jesus rose again from the dead, He was made so much better than the angels. What does this mean? God created mankind and made them a little lower than the angels, yet He set them over the works of His hands. Jesus, however, existing in the form of God, took on the form of man, and then paid the price of our sins. He was then raised up again to sit at the right hand of God and given a Name that is above all names—and was made so much better than the angels.

What does that mean for us? God became one with us in the flesh. And when Jesus was raised from the dead and was justified in the spirit, He was exalted up to the heavens again with angels and principalities and powers under His feet. Now, any born-again person has been exalted to that same position. Everyone who is in Christ has been exalted to the right hand of the Father!

Do you remember how Paul rebuked the Corinthian Christians for being carnal? He was pointing out that they were acting as though they were mere men, when in truth they were seated with Christ at the Father's right hand. In essence, he was saying, "You're better than the behavior you're exhibiting right now. You're not just mere men. You are the Body of Christ, seated in heavenly places with Him, and you are capable of so much more." (See 1 Corinthians chapter 3.)

> **1 Corinthians 15:25–28 (NKJV)**
>
> *For He must reign till He has put all enemies under His feet.*
>
> *The last enemy that will be destroyed is death.*
>
> *For "He has put all things under His feet." But when He says "all things are put under Him," it is evident that He who put all things under Him is excepted.*

CRUCIFIXION, DEATH, BURIAL, RESURRECTION AND ASCENSION

Now when all things are made subject to Him, then the Son Himself will also be subject to Him who put all things under Him, that God may be all in all.

According to this passage, all things are now under Jesus' feet. And as we saw earlier in this chapter, Jesus destroyed death and the power of death. Yet the Scriptures also say that death will be the last enemy that shall be destroyed. It sounds as though these verses contradict each other, but they do not. Here's how these Scriptures work together.

You see, the head of the Body—Jesus—has already overcome death. He has been resurrected and has ascended to Heaven. He will never face death again.

But the Body of Christ has not yet ascended to Heaven. Those who have died in the faith are awaiting the return of Jesus, when we will all be changed into His image. Those of us believers who are still alive right now will either one day physically die, or if we are alive when Jesus returns, then we shall be caught up in the air to be with Him (1 Corinthians 15:51–57; 1 Thessalonians 4:13–18).

So, for the Church, death's final sting will not be taken away fully until Jesus returns. The last enemy to be put under His feet—that is, put under the Body of Christ, the Church's feet—is physical death. The Head of the Church, Jesus, has already conquered death. The rest of the Body, which is the Church, will experience this victory after the second coming of Jesus. At that time, the Church will no longer suffer the death of our bodies. This is the last enemy to be done away with.

But right now, here is the good news: Every other enemy is already underneath our feet! Hallelujah!

We Share in What Jesus Did on the Cross

With that in mind, let's consider again Paul's prayer for the Ephesian Christians in Ephesians chapter 1.

> **Ephesians 1:17–23 (NKJV)**
> *… That the God of our Lord Jesus Christ, the Father of glory, may give to you the spirit of wisdom and revelation in the knowledge of Him,*
>
> *The eyes of your understanding being enlightened; that you may know what is the hope of His calling, what are the riches of the glory of His inheritance in the saints,*
>
> *And what is the exceeding greatness of His power toward us who believe, according to the working of His mighty power*
>
> *Which He worked in Christ when He raised Him from the dead and seated Him at His right hand in the heavenly places,*
>
> *Far above all principality and power and might and dominion, and every name that is named, not only in this age but also in that which is to come.*
>
> *And He put all things under His feet, and gave Him to be head over all things to the Church,*
>
> *Which is His Body, the fullness of Him who fills all in all.*

As Paul is praying for the Ephesian Christians, he says, "I want you to understand how great the power of God is toward you. It's the same power that was working in Christ when God the Father raised Him from the dead and seated Him at His right hand, far above all principality and power."

In other words, Paul wanted the Christians to understand that the same power that raised Jesus from the dead was at work in them too.

CRUCIFIXION, DEATH, BURIAL, RESURRECTION AND ASCENSION

The life-giving, healing, restoring power of the Holy Spirit is at work in our lives right now, as a result of the death, burial, and resurrection of Jesus Christ. This is what He accomplished on our behalf. He took away the curse of the Law and enabled us to sit in heavenly places with Him. By receiving Him as Savior and Lord, we are able to enjoy all that He won for us.

One day, our bodies will be made new just as our spirits are made new the moment we are born again. But right now, spiritually speaking, we are already seated with Him, because as believers, we are a part of His Body. The power and authority we have in and through Him is the same power and authority He has over all the principalities and powers He is seated above. Right now, as you read this sentence, we are seated in heavenly places with Him.

There are numerous Scriptures that clearly explain how we as believers share in all that Christ has experienced. First of all, by our faith in Him, we can say we were crucified with Him. We died with Him. We were buried with Him. The old version of you and me—the one that was trapped by the power of sin—is dead and buried with Christ.

Romans 6:3-4

Know ye not, that so many of us as were baptized into Jesus Christ were baptized into His death?

Therefore we are buried with Him by baptism into death: that like as Christ was raised up from the dead by the glory of the Father, even so we also should walk in newness of life.

Romans 6:6–7

Knowing this, that our old man is crucified with Him, that the body of sin might be destroyed, that henceforth we should not serve sin.

For he that is dead is freed from sin.

Colossians 3:3
For ye are dead, and your life is hid with Christ in God.

We Share in His Resurrection

Of course, the miracle of being born again is not just that we died with Christ, but that we were also raised up with Him into new life.

Romans 6:11
Likewise reckon ye also yourselves to be dead indeed unto sin, but alive unto God through Jesus Christ our Lord.

The lives you and I now live is by our faith in Him and all He accomplished for us through His crucifixion, death, burial, resurrection, and ascension. And it's not even our lives that we're living, but Christ's life being lived out in us.

Colossians 2:12
Buried with Him in baptism, wherein also ye are risen with Him through the faith of the operation of God, who hath raised Him from the dead.

2 Corinthians 5:17
Therefore if any man be in Christ, he is a new creature: old things are passed away;

CRUCIFIXION, DEATH, BURIAL, RESURRECTION AND ASCENSION

behold, all things are become new.

If you are in Christ, the old you is gone. You are a new creation in Christ! We were crucified with Him on the Cross, and now Christ lives through us. We share in both His death, which did away with sin, and His resurrection, which seated Him at God's right hand.

> **Colossians 1:12–15**
>
> *Giving thanks unto the Father, which hath made us meet to be partakers of the inheritance of the saints in light:*
>
> *Who hath delivered us from the power of darkness, and hath translated us into the kingdom of His dear Son.*
>
> *In whom we have redemption through His blood, even the forgiveness of sins:*
>
> *Who is the image of the invisible God, the firstborn of every creature.*

According to Colossians chapter 1, we have been delivered from the authority of darkness and translated into the Kingdom of Jesus Christ. As the first to be resurrected by God the Father, Jesus is the firstborn from the dead. But He's not the only person who would ever be resurrected. When Jesus rose again from the dead, we rose with Him. We share in the power of His resurrection when we are born again.

And that means that we are born after Him. We are born to new life, just as Jesus was, through our faith in Him. We are new creatures, in Him. We are part of His Kingdom now.

Satan No Longer Has Authority Over Us

Galatians 2:20
I am crucified with Christ: nevertheless I live; yet not I, but Christ liveth in me: and the life which I now live in the flesh I live by the faith of the Son of God, who loved me, and gave Himself for me.

As Paul explains in this verse, once we are born again, it is no longer us who live. The old "us" has died and been buried with Christ. The new "us" is a new creation. Christ is now living on the inside of us. He is our Head, and we are His Body.

This explains how it is that Satan has no authority over us anymore. Our old man, the former you and me, lived in the realm of sin, under the condemnation of the Law. But the old "us" that he had enslaved is now dead, because we are born again! When we are born again, we become a new person in Christ, one who is freed from the power of sin and death.

Our life is not our own; we belong to Christ. We're no longer subject to Satan. Satan no longer has authority over the believer. He's been condemned by God and stripped of all weapons against us. And we are free of him.

We Are Seated with Christ

Now, we know that Jesus sat down at the right hand of the Father when He rose from the dead. There are many passages of Scripture that describe the position of authority, power, and honor that Jesus holds.

Acts 2:33

Therefore being by the right hand of God exalted, and having received of the Father the promise of the Holy Ghost, He hath shed forth this, which ye now see and hear.

1 Peter 3:22

Who is gone into Heaven, and is on the right hand of God; angels and authorities and powers being made subject unto Him.

Through this position of honor at the Father's right hand, Jesus is exalted above all. Angels, demons, humans—we are all under His rulership and subject to Him.

1 Corinthians 15:25–28

For He must reign, till He hath put all enemies under His feet.

The last enemy that shall be destroyed is death.

For He hath put all things under His feet. But when He saith all things are put under Him, it is manifest that He is excepted, which did put all things under Him.

And when all things shall be subdued unto Him, then shall the Son also Himself be subject unto Him that put all things under Him, that God may be all in all.

As Jesus sits at the right hand of the Father, all the angels and demons are under His feet. He is waiting for all things to be brought under control. What is the last enemy that will be subdued? First Corinthians 15:26 says the last enemy that will be put under Jesus' feet is death.

But didn't Jesus already defeat death when He rose from the dead? Yes, He did! Hebrews 2:14–15 says that Jesus destroyed *him who had the power of death, that is, the devil.* Second Timothy 1:10 (NKJV) says, *But has now been revealed by the appearing of our Savior Jesus Christ, who has abolished death and brought life and immortality to light through the Gospel.*

If we combine these two passages, we can see that Jesus destroyed the one who had the power of death and also abolished or destroyed death itself. When He rose again from the dead, Jesus literally destroyed death!

Jesus destroyed death when He rose from the dead, but He is still waiting for the day when death no longer affects His Body, the Church. The Church is His Body, and Christ is the head of the Church. Until His Second Coming, those of us who are alive can still die in our physical bodies. The power of death over us is destroyed, but our bodies can still die. This will not change until Jesus' Second Coming.

But there's coming a day when you and I are going to be changed. We will receive a new body, and death will be abolished.

1 Corinthians 15:51–52

Behold, I shew you a mystery; We shall not all sleep, but we shall all be changed,

In a moment, in the twinkling of an eye, at the last trump: for the trumpet shall sound, and the dead shall be raised incorruptible, and we shall be changed.

When we receive our new, resurrection bodies, death will be conquered completely under Jesus' feet. But until then, we as the Church are still living in what many call the Age of Grace—the period between Jesus' resurrection from the dead and the Rapture of the Church, before His Second Coming. In the period we are now living in, all author-

CRUCIFIXION, DEATH, BURIAL, RESURRECTION AND ASCENSION

ity is given unto Jesus, and the devil and the angels are under His control.

And He has delegated His authority to the Church to use in the Earth as we await His return and preach the Gospel.

The Holy Spirit Within Us

Romans 8:11
But if the Spirit of Him that raised up Jesus from the dead dwell in you, He that raised up Christ from the dead shall also quicken your mortal bodies by His Spirit that dwelleth in you.

The Spirit that raised Jesus from the dead—the Holy Spirit—is dwelling in you right now. He is the One who helps us in this life to have victory over the things of the flesh, the evil of the devil, and death.

Ephesians 1:13–14
In whom ye also trusted, after that ye heard the word of truth, the Gospel of your salvation: in whom also after that ye believed, ye were sealed with that holy Spirit of promise,

Which is the earnest of our inheritance until the redemption of the purchased possession, unto the praise of His glory.

The Holy Spirit is given to us as a down payment, as proof that God owns us now. The Spirit is our evidence and guarantee that we belong to God until the redemption of the purchased possession—until we are with Him forever. Now, the term used in this Scripture is translated into English as "the earnest of our inheritance." Earnest money is the down payment needed to guarantee that a house you want to purchase will be yours as the contract is being worked out. Once the contract comes through, you take full possession of the house.

This is the picture Paul gives us of the role of the Holy Spirit in our lives. Jesus purchased us with His blood, and He put a down payment inside of us—the Holy Spirit. The Holy Spirit is a sign to Satan and the world that we belong to God. He is the down payment until He brings us to Himself, either after our physical death, or during the Rapture, whichever comes first.

Our bodies belong to God. Our spirit is born again into the Kingdom of God. Our minds are being renewed. The Holy Spirit is evidence of this.

Remember that in Ephesians 1, as we discussed earlier, the Apostle Paul prays for Christians, that our eyes would be opened to see the exceeding greatness of God's power toward us, the same power that raised Christ from the dead.

We are to see and understand that Jesus destroyed the power of Satan over us. Satan was judged and condemned through the Cross, and the primary weapon he used—the condemnation of the Law—was taken away.

Jesus then translated us through His death, burial, and resurrection into His Kingdom, delivering us from the authority of darkness. Our spirits are now born again. It is no longer us who live, but Christ living in us. He put His Holy Spirit in us as a sign to Satan that says, "Keep your hands off My property." It's also a reminder that one day our bodies will be changed as well.

CRUCIFIXION, DEATH, BURIAL, RESURRECTION AND ASCENSION

Put a big sign on your heart that says, "No Trespassing!" When sickness tries to come against you, when Satan tries to come at you with fear and doubt, say, "No trespassing, Satan!" We don't belong to the devil, and he has no right to enter into our lives with sickness, fear, lack, or any other evil thing.

Philippians 3:20 (NKJV)
For our citizenship is in Heaven, from which we also eagerly wait for the Savior, the Lord Jesus Christ.

Never forget that you are a member of Christ's Body, the Church, and a citizen of Heaven. Through the power of the Cross, you no longer belong to Satan, and he no longer has a right to rule over you. This is the cornerstone of the foundation of the authority you have in Christ!

CHAPTER 7

AUTHORITY REGAINED

The curse of the Law, which includes sickness and lack, belongs to the realm of sin, and Satan operates within this realm. When sin dominated our lives, Satan was able to use the full force of the curse of the Law to control us. Once Jesus paid the full penalty for our sins, however, the power of the curse was broken, and our condemnation was removed. Because Jesus took away the condemnation of the Law, He took away Satan's right over our lives.

Ephesians 1:18–23, our foundational Scripture for this book, says Jesus was raised from the dead and seated at God the Father's right hand, *far above all principality, and power, and might, and dominion, and every name that is named.* All things are now under Jesus' feet!

> **Colossians 2:15**
> *And having spoiled principalities and powers, He (Jesus) made a shew of them openly, triumphing over them in it.*

Not only is Jesus seated at God's right hand, but through His death and resurrection, He also disarmed Satan, defeating the devil's principalities and powers. We now have authority over Satan because he lost all authority by unjustly condemning the sinless Christ to death on the Cross.

Romans 8:3-4

For what the Law could not do, in that it was weak through the flesh, God sending His own Son in the likeness of sinful flesh, and for sin, condemned sin in the flesh:

That the righteousness of the Law might be fulfilled in us, who walk not after the flesh, but after the Spirit.

As Christians, we walk after the Spirit now, not the flesh. It is by faith in Christ that we are counted as righteous in His eyes. Through this righteousness, we have great spiritual power and authority available to us.

Colossians 1:20–22

And, having made peace through the blood of His Cross, by Him to reconcile all things unto Himself; by Him, I say, whether they be things in Earth, or things in Heaven.

And you, that were sometime alienated and enemies in your mind by wicked works, yet now hath He reconciled

In the body of His flesh through death, to present you holy and unblameable and unreproveable in His sight.

So, we see again that through the blood Jesus shed on the Cross, He has forgiven us and presented us to God the Father as holy in His sight. This act of forgiveness and the restoration of our holiness gives us authority over the devil, because he only had authority due to our sinful state and our enslavement to him. We were once slaves to sin.

But we are slaves no more! Jesus took care of our sin. He accepted the penalty of the Law that condemned us. We are condemned no more.

What If a Christian Sins?

This question is a common one among born-again believers. Obviously, no person is perfect, even after we receive Jesus as our Lord and Savior. Our spirits may be reborn through faith in Christ, but our souls—our mind, will, and emotions—are being renewed day by day through the washing of the Word of God (2 Corinthians 4:16; Ephesians 5:26–27). So, there will be times when we make mistakes, give in to old ways of thinking, or fail to be Christlike in our words or actions.

For this purpose, God placed 1 John 1:9 in the Bible.

> **1 John 1:9**
> *If we confess our sins, He is faithful and just to forgive us our sins, and to cleanse us from all unrighteousness.*

This verse is a reassurance to you and me that the daily mistakes we make can be dealt with through repentance and the shed blood of Jesus. As Christians, our trust is never in ourselves—it is always in Jesus and His sacrifice. Even if you and I sin, we have no fear of condemnation. The blood of Jesus speaks for us before God's throne continually.

And because Jesus says you're righteous, you are! Your sins are forgiven, and you have been set free from slavery to Satan.

> **Colossians 1:13–14 (NKJV)**
> *He has delivered us from the power of darkness and conveyed us into the kingdom of the Son of His love,*

In whom we have redemption through His blood, the forgiveness of sins.

Jesus took us out of Satan's kingdom and placed us in the Kingdom of God instead. There is such freedom in knowing that our righteousness does not depend on us, but on Jesus—who is always perfect and will never let us down or forsake us.

Romans 6:17–18 (NKJV)
But God be thanked that though you were slaves of sin, yet you obeyed from the heart that form of doctrine to which you were delivered.

And having been set free from sin, you became slaves of righteousness.

When we believed in the Word of God that was preached to us as sinners, and we put our faith in Christ, we were made free from sin. We're no longer slaves to sin, but now we are slaves to righteousness. We went from Satan's slaves to being Jesus' slaves.

The blood of Jesus never stops speaking for us. We can keep our faith in His blood and be forgiven continually. As slaves to Christ, Christians serve a Good Master.

Remember—in Christ, we are no longer condemned (Romans 8:1–2). But if we don't know we are free from condemnation, we can easily be taken in by a tactic that the devil finds useful against many Christians. He accuses us and tries to lead us into feeling condemned, thus causing us to doubt our authority over him.

Revelation 12:10–11
And I heard a loud voice saying in heaven, Now is come salvation, and strength, and the Kingdom of our God, and the power of His Christ: for the accuser of our brethren is

cast down, which accused them before our God day and night.

And they overcame him by the blood of the Lamb, and by the word of their testimony; and they loved not their lives unto the death.

Never forget that Satan is called *the accuser of the brethren*. Of course, this verse will find its fulfillment when Jesus returns to Earth, and Satan is finally thrown into utter darkness. One day, he will no longer be able to accuse us before God.

Until he is thrown into the Lake of Fire, however, Satan accuses us before God every day and points out our imperfections. His ultimate goal is to keep men and women living in this natural realm under the condemnation of the Law. He hopes that we will believe the accusations and surrender again to his will.

How are Christians to overcome Satan's accusations? Through the blood of the Lamb and the word of our testimony! It is the blood of Jesus that makes us righteous. By speaking your testimony—which is essentially your confession that the Gospel is true—you're speaking faith in the blood of Jesus to save you. You're testifying about who you are in Christ! And the fact that you are in Christ is why Satan has no authority over your life.

Remember, Jesus has delivered us from the power of darkness. Through Christ, we have been translated from the kingdom of darkness into the kingdom of light—the Kingdom of Jesus Christ! In Colossians 1:13, when Paul says Jesus delivered us from the *power* of darkness, the word *power* in the original Greek actually means *authority*. He delivered us from the authority of darkness. Satan has no authority over a born-again believer!

Jesus disarmed, or took away, Satan's weapons, including the condemnation of the Law against us. Now, we can overcome the accusations by the blood of the Lamb!

We've been translated from the kingdom of darkness into the Kingdom of Jesus Christ. This rescue was made possible through His life and death.

> **Galatians 2:20**
> *I am crucified with Christ: nevertheless I live; yet not I, but Christ liveth in me: and the life which I now live in the flesh I live by the faith of the Son of God, who loved me, and gave Himself for me.*

> **Matthew 28:18**
> *And Jesus came and spake unto them, saying, All power is given unto Me in Heaven and in Earth.*

All power and authority are given unto Jesus now. What Adam lost, Jesus regained. When we become born again, we come under Jesus' authority.

We Do Not Need to Fear the Devil

If you are a Christian for any length of time, you will either experience the attack of the enemy in your life, or you will see it in the lives of other Christians. Why does this happen? And why do some Christians succumb to these attacks?

Christians get in trouble when they do not know how to exercise their authority in Christ. Remember, sin has been dealt with on the

AUTHORITY REGAINED

Cross, but Satan has not yet been thrown into the pit of Hell. He is still active in the Earth today, resisting the work of God and those who belong to God. Satan will try to attack our bodies with sickness and our minds with oppression. His goal is to keep us from doing what God has called us to do.

When anything evil comes against you—whether it is cancer or some other sickness, or any other evil thing—you have the authority as a believer to kick it out of your life. Satan and his demons are under Jesus' feet, which means they are under our feet too. The only way Satan can gain power over a Christian is through deception, making us believe in his power, making us afraid of him.

The opposite of faith is fear. And fear is actually a perverted form of faith, because fearing is believing—it's just believing the wrong thing! If you fear the lies of Satan, it means you believe Satan has more power than God. However, if you fear (or revere) God and trust in His power above all else, you will not fear man or Satan. Why is there no longer a need for Christians to fear the devil? The book of Hebrews explains.

> **Hebrews 2:14–15**
> *Forasmuch then as the children are partakers of flesh and blood, He also Himself likewise took part of the same; that through death He might destroy him that had the power of death, that is, the devil;*
>
> *And deliver them who through fear of death were all their lifetime subject to bondage.*

First of all, we do not need to fear the devil because Jesus destroyed his power over us. Yes, the devil is still around. He still operates in the Earth. But Jesus destroyed his power and authority over everyone who is in Christ.

> **2 Timothy 1:10**
>
> *But is now made manifest by the appearing of our Saviour Jesus Christ, who hath abolished death, and hath brought life and immortality to light through the Gospel.*

Second, Jesus also abolished or destroyed death. He overcame it, and we will overcome it in the end, when Jesus returns. Thus, there is no need for a believer to fear death.

> **Revelation 1:18**
>
> *I am He that liveth, and was dead; and, behold, I am alive for evermore, Amen; and have the keys of hell and of death.*

Jesus now holds the keys of Hell and death. Keys represent authority. When you have a key to a car, that means you have the authority to use that car. If you have a key to your house or a key to a lock, you are the one who has the authority to open it and use what is inside. So, Jesus has all authority in Heaven and on Earth, and He has authority over Hell and death.

With this knowledge, I have two questions for you to consider: If Jesus defeated Satan and took away his authority, why is Satan still operating in the Earth? Why does he continue to resist the Lord when he cannot win in the end?

I believe the answer is that Satan knows his days are short. One might say he's like a criminal who has been sentenced to death for his crimes. Satan knows that one day soon, he will suffer eternal punishment for his crimes. But in the meantime, he's still wreaking destruction—even though he's condemned and stripped of his rights! The great news, however, is that he will be thrown into the lake of fire one day. When that day comes, Satan will never trouble or torment God's children ever again.

So, why does Satan seem to have so much power and influence in the world today? One reason is that everything Jesus did for us must be received by faith.

> **John 3:16**
> *For God so loved the world, that He gave his only begotten Son, that whosoever believeth in Him should not perish, but have everlasting life.*

The phrase *whosoever believes in Him* means it's up to you and me to accept or reject what Jesus did for us.

When we are born again, we receive the benefits of everything Jesus did for us—which includes being freed from Satan's authority. However, those who refuse to believe in Jesus are still under Satan's authority, which is one reason he is still able to operate in the Earth.

While Satan's authority over all who believe in Christ has been taken away by Christ, he still can have influence in the life of an unbeliever—and he can only operate through humans in this Earth. Satan blinds the minds of unbelievers through religions, philosophy, and other things that cause people to believe lies.

> **2 Corinthians 4:3–7**
> *But if our Gospel be hid, it is hid to them that are lost:*
>
> *In whom the god of this world hath blinded the minds of them which believe not, lest the light of the glorious Gospel of Christ, who is the image of God, should shine unto them.*

> *For we preach not ourselves, but Christ Jesus the Lord; and ourselves your servants for Jesus' sake.*
>
> *For God, who commanded the light to shine out of darkness, hath shined in our hearts, to give the light of the knowledge of the glory of God in the face of Jesus Christ.*
>
> *But we have this treasure in earthen vessels, that the excellency of the power may be of God, and not of us.*

Another reason Satan is still at work today is that the Church is not always exercising the authority Jesus has given us. The Lord has given us so much more authority and power than most Christians understand or live out. Throughout Church history, little glimpses of this authority can be seen through the mighty men and women of God who learned to exercise it with great results: the sick healed, dead raised, and demons cast out.

Over the years, we have seen whole nations changed as a result of Christians learning to exercise their authority in Christ. For example, a group of pastors living in the former communist state of East Germany got ahold of Brother Kenneth E. Hagin's book, *The Believer's Authority*. They began to use their authority in Christ during their prayer time. They called on God's Kingdom to advance in their part of the world.

The Berlin Wall came down, and these pastors were able to spread the Gospel message throughout Eastern Europe. I was told by a missionary friend that in that area today, the number one Christian author in some of those former Communist countries is Kenneth E. Hagin. It was the message of the authority of the believer that helped change those nations.

The Devil Has Been Stripped of His Power

Colossians 2:15
And having spoiled principalities and powers, he made a shew of them openly, triumphing over them in it..

This Scripture reveals the key to how we have authority over the devil and all his works. We have talked about this in chapter 6, but let me say it again: Through the Cross, Jesus satisfied the demands of the Law. In doing so, He stripped the enemy, his principalities and powers, of their authority over us.

The word *spoiled* in the original Greek language means to disarm or take away weapons. It literally means to strip someone both of weapons and clothes, leaving them naked. This is how the devil and his demons have been dealt with. They have been stripped of their weapons against us, which was prophesied in the Book of Isaiah.

Isaiah 54:17
No weapon that is formed against thee shall prosper; and every tongue that shall rise against thee in judgment thou shalt condemn. This is the heritage of the servants of the Lord, and their righteousness is of Me, saith the Lord.

Revelation 12:9–11 (NKJV)
So the great dragon was cast out, that serpent of old, called the Devil and Satan, who deceives the whole world; he was cast to the Earth, and his angels were cast out with him.

Then I heard a loud voice saying in heaven, "Now salvation, and strength, and the King-

> dom of our God, and the power of His Christ have come, for the accuser of our brethren, who accused them before our God day and night, has been cast down.
>
> And they overcame him by the blood of the Lamb and by the word of their testimony, and they did not love their lives to the death.

Notice that this Scripture passage refers to Satan as *the serpent*. In fact, it calls him *that serpent of old*. This hearkens back to the Garden of Eden and the fall of man, when the serpent lied to Adam and Eve and caused them to sin against God.

A little later in this passage, Satan is referred to as *the accuser*. And then these verses explain how Christians overcome the accuser, which we have mentioned already—through the blood of the Lamb and the word of our testimonies. Yes, Satan accuses us of sins, mistakes, and flaws, but the blood of Jesus speaks as well—it speaks on our behalf. While we were sinners, Christ died for us and made us righteous by His blood. Because of the blood, Christians are saved from wrath and judgment. The blood declares our forgiveness and redemption continually!

How does the blood of Jesus overcome Satan? Through Jesus' death on the Cross, Satan lost his ability to condemn us because of sin. Satan brought condemnation and accusation against us, but on the Cross, Jesus satisfied the demands of the Law. The blood Jesus shed still speaks today. It says, "You're not condemned! You're not cursed! You don't deserve to go to Hell, because of what Jesus did for you!" When Jesus nailed the Law to the Cross, He forever took away Satan's ability to condemn you.

It was sin that brought us under Satan's authority, but Jesus became sin for us. He took on the curse of the Law for us while He was on the

Cross. We are now made righteous by His blood—freed from slavery to sin—through faith in Jesus Christ. It is not because of what you and I did, but because of what Jesus did, that we are free of Satan's power.

The Open Defeat of Satan

Colossians 2:15 (NKJV)
Having disarmed principalities and powers, He made a public spectacle of them, triumphing over them in it.

The shed blood of Jesus has freed us from the tyranny of Satan and made us slaves (or servants) to the righteousness of God. This spiritual fact is no longer a secret or a mystery. Now, it is open knowledge. Not only did Jesus spoil or strip the devil of his authority over us, but He also made an open display of His triumph over the devil, and the devil's defeat.

In this verse, the apostle Paul used language familiar to the Colossian people whom he was writing to. Colossae was a small city in Asia Minor that was under the control of Rome, the empire that ruled the whole area from the Middle East all the way up into Europe, and even the Northern part of Africa.

Rome was incredibly powerful and had a strong army. When the Roman army came into a country or city such as Colossae, they would conquer the city and capture its king or leader, along with all of the people within the local government. The Romans would strip the king or leader naked, put him in chains, and march him through the city streets. The Roman leader who conquered the city would ride on horseback behind the captured king and all the prisoners so everyone could see it. The captives would be publicly shamed and humiliated, while the Roman leader openly declared his victory over his enemy.

In a similar fashion, Jesus defeated Satan through His death on the Cross and then led Satan in a public show of humiliation and disgrace, openly shaming both Satan and his demons. The devil and all the demons who fell with him were paraded around all of Heaven and Hell, which was Jesus' way of declaring, "I have utterly defeated you."

> **1 Corinthians 2:7–8 (NKJV)**
>
> *But we speak the wisdom of God in a mystery, the hidden wisdom which God ordained before the ages for our glory,*
>
> *Which none of the rulers of this age knew; for had they known, they would not have crucified the Lord of glory.*

Satan thought his plan to defeat Jesus was successful all the way up until his defeat. Through Jesus' death on the Cross, Satan was judged and found guilty, while humanity was freed from judgment. In other words, Satan came underneath the judgment of God, while humanity came out from under judgment.

> **Colossians 1:20–22 (NKJV)**
>
> *And by Him to reconcile all things to Himself, by Him, whether things on Earth or things in heaven, having made peace through the blood of His Cross.*
>
> *And you, who once were alienated and enemies in your mind by wicked works, yet now He has reconciled*
>
> *In the body of His flesh through death, to present you holy, and blameless, and above reproach in His sight.*

> **Ephesians 2:15–16 (NKJV)**
>
> *Having abolished in His flesh the enmity, that is, the law of commandments contained in ordinances, so as to create in Himself one new man from the two, thus making peace,*
>
> *And that He might reconcile them both to God in one Body through the Cross, thereby putting to death the enmity.*

Jesus has made us righteous in His sight and called us His own. Through the blood of His Cross, He reconciled us with God. This means Satan, the accuser, has no authority anymore to condemn you or come against you. In John 16, Jesus said Satan, the prince of this world, was coming, but he had no right over Jesus' life. Christians can say the same thing as Jesus did, because He fulfilled the requirements of the Law to make us righteous. Satan may try to come against us, but he has no authority over our lives. It doesn't matter whether you and I are perfect—we overcome by the blood of Jesus! Faith in the blood of Jesus makes us righteous, and nothing Satan says can condemn us.

> **Romans 8:1 (NKJV)**
>
> *There is therefore now no condemnation to those who are in Christ Jesus, who do not walk according to the flesh, but according to the Spirit.*

There is no condemnation for those who are in Christ. As we walk in the Spirit and walk in faith, the blood of Jesus has declared and continues to declare us righteous. Like Jesus, you and I can say, "Satan has no authority in my life."

> **Hebrews 2:14–15 (NKJV)**
>
> *Inasmuch then as the children have partaken of flesh and blood, He Himself likewise*

shared in the same, that through death He might destroy him who had the power of death, that is, the devil,

And release those who through fear of death were all their lifetime subject to bondage.

Jesus destroyed Satan, but that doesn't mean he's not still on the Earth, trying to cause trouble in the lives of those who are unsaved or those Christians who don't know their authority in the Lord. Yes, Satan is already judged, and his destiny is sealed—he will end up in the lake of fire. In the meantime, as believers, we are not in his kingdom, so Satan has no authority over our lives. On the contrary, Jesus told us to cast out devils and take authority over him and his works.

Authority Is Ours Again Through Christ

Adam was given authority over the Earth, but Satan came and lied to Eve. When Adam and Eve didn't exercise their authority, they surrendered their authority to Satan. This action is what made us all Satan's slaves. God, however, promised Adam and Eve the hope of freedom through the Seed of Woman.

Adam made all of humanity slaves to sin with no authority, but Jesus was the prophesied Seed of the Woman. Jesus was a man with no sin. Thus, Satan had no authority over Him. Jesus came to the sons of Adam, who were under the bondage of sin and disease. By stretching His hand toward mankind, Jesus offered humanity freedom. Satan couldn't stop Him—not even when he came up with the plan for Christ's crucifixion.

Satan's plan to crucify Jesus and keep humanity in bondage was foiled. Jesus took our sin and judgment upon Himself. The condemnation of the Law was put upon Jesus—He became sin and took on the curse for us. Jesus died, but He didn't stay in the grave! Three days later, Jesus rose from the dead, overcoming death. He didn't rise up again as sin or the curse, but as the righteousness of God. He overcame sin and death.

I cannot say this enough: Christians are now free from Satan's tyranny. Satan is condemned, and he's under our feet!

Matthew 28:18–19 (NKJV)

And Jesus came and spoke to them saying, "All authority has been given to Me in heaven and on earth.

Go therefore and make disciples of all the nations, baptizing them in the name of the Father and of the Son and of the Holy Spirit.

Jesus was given all authority in Heaven and Earth. He gave all of that authority back to Christians. Armed with the authority that has been restored to us, we are to preach the Gospel throughout the world.

Walk Out Your Authority in Christ Every Day

1 Corinthians 15:22–27 (NKJV)

For as in Adam all die, even so in Christ all shall be made alive.

But each one in his own order: Christ the firstfruits, afterward those who are Christ's at His coming.

Then comes the end, when He delivers the kingdom to God the Father, when He puts an end to all rule and all authority and power.

For He must reign till He has put all enemies under His feet.

The last enemy that will be destroyed is death.

For "He has put all things under His feet." But when He says "all things are put under Him," it is evident that He who put all things under Him is excepted.

Paul told us in Ephesians that when Jesus rose from the dead, all principalities and powers, Satan and all of his demons, were put under Jesus' feet. But it is a process that is still being worked out day by day. Evil and wickedness are still in the world, but Jesus is bringing everything to a state where He will be King of all the kingdoms of the Earth.

This is why we as believers must learn the extent of our authority in Christ and how to exercise that authority successfully in the Earth. As we do, we will see victories in our own lives. We will see the Word of God change the lives of people around us. And we will see the Gospel spread throughout the world, for God's glory.

CHAPTER 8

THE NAME AND WHAT IT MEANS

Wherefore God also hath highly exalted Him, and given Him a Name which is above every name:

That at the Name of Jesus every knee should bow, of things in heaven, and things in earth, and things under the earth.

— Philippians 2:9–10

When Jesus was raised from the dead, His Name became more powerful than ever. When Jesus ascended on high, God put everything under His feet, so He reigns supreme. Like a conquering king or emperor, His Name is now the name that rules over everything He conquered—including the devil and every evil work. His Name has authority in Heaven and in Earth—even in Hell, which is under the Earth.

The Name of Jesus is so much more powerful than many of us realize. And according to the Bible, He received that Name in three ways—by *inheritance,* by *conquest,* and by *bestowal.*

Hebrews 1:4–5 (NIV)
So He became as much superior to the angels as the Name He has inherited is superior to theirs.

For to which of the angels did God ever say, "You are My Son; today I have become Your Father"? Or again, "I will be His Father, and He will be my Son"?

This passage of Scripture describes what took place when He rose from the dead. That's when He was called the first begotten from the dead. At that time, He received a Name through inheritance. If you inherit something through your birthright, your inheritance comes through your right as a member of your family.

Jesus is the firstborn from the dead, and we know He was born again into that righteousness, thus securing our new birth. By inheritance as a member of God's family, then, Jesus received the Name that is more powerful than any other. All of this authority is given to the Body of Christ as an inheritance too, because Jesus became the firstborn of the dead. And we are also members of the family of God, through our faith in Him.

The second way Jesus received His Name is through His victory over Satan. He's a conqueror. Ephesians 1:19–20 tells us that God's power raised Jesus from the dead and set Him over all principalities and powers. In other words, Jesus conquered Satan, and through His conquest, He received His Name—much like many ancient cultures where a king would conquer a people and receive a name that acknowledged their victory. Now, Satan and all the demons in the world acknowledge Jesus as the Son of God.

The third way Jesus received a Name that is above all others is by bestowal. Father God gave it to Him as a reward for His victory. If you've studied history, for example, you've probably heard of Alexander the Great or Genghis Khan because of their epic conquests. Names like "the Great" and "Khan" (which means "king" or "chief") have often been bestowed when a person overcomes an enemy. That name is a sign of honor and respect. Jesus triumphed over Satan, nailing our sins to the Cross, and stripped Satan of his weapons. When God raised Jesus from the dead, He therefore gave Him a Name that has power in Heaven, Earth, and Hell.

And just as Jesus received a Name above all names, He gave the disciples—and all who follow after Him today—the right to use His Name, and the awesome authority it holds. The use of His Name is a bestowal of rights, privileges, and authorities. There is no other name like the Name of Jesus! It is powerful!

Now, a name means nothing if not for the person behind the name. In other words, the name is only as important as the person who has that name. For example, when the President of the United States comes to town, all kinds of preparations take place because of his visit. The streets are blocked and the buildings are secured—all because of a title. However, one day even the President will bow his knee and say, "Jesus is Lord."

The man behind the Name of Jesus is the One who lived a sinless life and fulfilled the Law for us. He's the One who took our sin, shame, and sickness away. Jesus took away the judgment against us, the very thing that kept us separated from God, going to Hell in our place. His sacrifice broke the power of sin, death, and Hell over our lives.

Jesus conquered Satan and all his demons, putting them under His feet. Now, He sits at the right hand of the Father God. One day soon, He's coming back for us. No wonder His name has power!

And never forget, Jesus said, "I give you My Name." He told us to go preach in His Name, to teach the nations in His Name, and to do miracles in His Name. We have His permission to cast out devils, raise the dead, and heal the sick in His Name. Our authority is found in the Name of Jesus. Let's begin to exercise it!

We Have the Right to Use His Name

Matthew 28:18–20 (NKJV)

And Jesus came and spoke to them, saying, "All authority has been given to Me in Heaven and on Earth.

Go therefore and make disciples of all the nations, baptizing them in the Name of the Father and of the Son and of the Holy Spirit,

Teaching them to observe all things that I have commanded you; and lo, I am with you always, even to the end of the age."

All authority was given to Christ when He was raised from the dead. Christ then delegated to us His authority to use in the Earth as we pursue the work of His Kingdom.

Mark 16:15–18 (NKJV)

And He said to them, "Go into all the world and preach the Gospel to every creature.

He who believes and is baptized will be saved; but he who does not believe will be condemned.

And these signs will follow those who believe: In My name they will cast out demons; they will speak with new tongues;

They will take up serpents; and if they drink anything deadly, it will by no means hurt them; they will lay hands on the sick, and they will recover."

Jesus said, "Go in My Name to spread the Gospel, and I will back you up with the power of Heaven. You will destroy the works of Satan, just as I destroyed the works of Satan." We can do so because He has given us authority in His Name. (For a refresher on how delegated authority works, review the story of the Roman Centurion in chapter 4 of this book.)

> **Matthew 16:18–19 (NKJV)**
> *And I also say to you that you are Peter, and on this rock I will build My Church, and the gates of Hades shall not prevail against it.*
>
> *And I will give you the keys of the Kingdom of Heaven, and whatever you bind on Earth will be bound in Heaven, and whatever you loose on Earth will be loosed in Heaven.*

Jesus said, "I'm building My Church," which is His Body—a supernatural race—"and the gates of Hell will not prevail against it." Satan cannot prevail against us unless we allow him to do so. Whatever we bind on Earth shall be bound in Heaven, and whatever we loose on Earth shall be loosed in Heaven. If the Church uses faith and the Name of Jesus to declare God's will in the Earth, it will happen. If the Church doesn't allow something, it won't happen. However, if the Church allows it, it will happen. Authority belongs to the Church—not Satan.

If the Church as a whole would unite in faith—if we would realize our authority in Christ and use it in a united effort—we could have a much greater influence on the world for the sake of the Gospel. The gates of Hell will not prevail against us.

And when the Bible talks about the gates of Hell, keep this in mind: Gates are not an offensive weapon. They are defensive. Their job is to trap unsaved, oppressed people as prisoners of Hell, and to keep the

Church outside, where we can't make a difference and set people free.

However, Jesus said those gates cannot withstand the Church. We have the authority to bust down the gates of Hell and free the souls that are bound.

Sent Forth in His Name

When Jesus rose from the dead, He sent out His believers into all the world to preach the Gospel and represent His Kingdom to the world. He now has the Name above all names, and with this Name comes authority in Heaven, on Earth, and under the Earth, or Hell. He then told us, "Go in My Name, and do the works of God."

What does this look like, in practice? We can get an idea of what Jesus intended from what His disciples experienced during His earthly ministry. Remember, even before He was crucified, He sent out His disciples to do the works of God. Their experiences show us what was to come in all its fullness after Jesus rose from the dead and delegated His authority to us, His Body, in the Earth.

Let's look at what the disciples experienced when Jesus sent them forth in His Name to use His authority and share the Kingdom of God.

> **Matthew 10:1, 7–8**
>
> *And when He had called unto Him His twelve disciples, He gave them power against unclean spirits, to cast them out, and to heal all manner of sickness and all manner of disease.*
>
> *And as ye go, preach, saying, The Kingdom of Heaven is at hand.*
>
> *Heal the sick, cleanse the lepers, raise the dead, cast out devils: freely ye have received,*

freely give.

Here, we see that when Jesus sent the twelve disciples to preach the Gospel, He instructed them to do more than talk about Him. He also told them to heal the sick, cast out devils, and even raise the dead. It is clear that He expected them to do mighty works and to experience miracles as an essential part of ministering in His Name. There is nothing in this passage of Scripture that makes healing, deliverance, and other miracles seem unusual. They are not meant to be the exceptions to the rule.

No, miracles *are* the rule. We can and should expect them to take place when we minister in Jesus' Name.

In another instance, Jesus sent out seventy disciples. Notice what their experience was.

Luke 10:1, 17
After these things the Lord appointed other seventy also, and sent them two and two before His face into every city and place, whither He Himself would come.

And the seventy returned again with joy, saying, Lord, even the devils are subject unto us through Thy Name.

In both of these instances, Jesus sent out His disciples, expecting them to do miracles and accomplish God's will. And in both instances, miracles took place. Why? Because His Name had—and still has—power. His Name has the authority of Heaven behind it.

Yes, you read that correctly. Even before Jesus rose from the dead, His Name had authority, because He was without sin—and therefore, He was not subject to the authority of the devil. After He was raised from the dead, He was given the Name above every other name—overcoming sin, sickness, death, and Satan. What the disciples experienced before His victory is now available in its fullness to every believer, because of what Jesus accomplished for us on the Cross—if only we will learn to walk in it.

The Authority of Every Believer

Luke 10:18–20

And He said unto them, I beheld Satan as lightning fall from Heaven.

Behold, I give unto you power to tread on serpents and scorpions, and over all the power of the enemy: and nothing shall by any means hurt you.

Notwithstanding in this rejoice not, that the spirits are subject unto you; but rather rejoice, because your names are written in Heaven.

When Jesus said He gave us *power*, the word He used actually means *authority*. Jesus gave us power, or authority, to crush beneath our feet all the power of the enemy. This means every believer—including you and me—has authority over Satan.

Mark 16:15–20 (NKJV)

And He said to them, "Go into all the world and preach the Gospel to every creature.

He who believes and is baptized will be saved; but he who does not believe will be condemned.

And these signs will follow those who believe: In My name they will cast out demons; they will speak with new tongues;

They will take up serpents; and if they drink anything deadly, it will by no means hurt them; they will lay hands on the sick, and they will recover."

So then, after the Lord had spoken to them, He was received up into Heaven, and sat down at the right hand of God.

And they went out and preached everywhere, the Lord working with them and confirming the word through the accompanying signs.

The mandate Jesus gave in Luke 10:18–20 before His resurrection is essentially the same mandate He gave to all believers, the Church, His Body, after His resurrection. Now, we can walk in that authority, using His Name to reign in the Earth.

Before Jesus was crucified, He gave the disciples authority. With that authority, they cast out devils, healed the sick, and raised the dead. After Jesus was resurrected, He gave everyone who believes in Him authority. This is what the Scriptures mean by the phrase *signs following*. Jesus didn't say signs only followed apostles, prophets, and preachers. No! Signs, wonders, and miracles follow those who believe in Him. That's the entire Body of Christ—including you and me!

If you are a believer in Jesus Christ, then you should expect these signs to follow you. And you should command the devil to depart, in Jesus' Name, whenever you see him trying to cause trouble.

Greater Works Shall You Do

We are to do the works Jesus did during His ministry on Earth. What are those works?

> **Luke 4:16–21 (NKJV)**
>
> *So He came to Nazareth, where He had been brought up. And as His custom was, He went into the synagogue on the Sabbath day, and stood up to read.*
>
> *And He was handed the book of the prophet Isaiah. And when He had opened the book, He found the place where it was written:*
>
> *"The Spirit of the Lord is upon Me, because He has anointed Me to preach the Gospel to the poor; He has sent Me to heal the brokenhearted, to proclaim liberty to the captives and recovery of sight to the blind, to set at liberty those who are oppressed;*
>
> *To proclaim the acceptable year of the Lord."*
>
> *Then He closed the book, and gave it back to the attendant and sat down. And the eyes of all who were in the synagogue were fixed on Him.*
>
> *And He began to say to them, "Today this Scripture is fulfilled in your hearing."*

Jesus fulfilled this mission—preaching, healing, delivering, and setting free those in need. And in John 14, He tells us we can do this and more.

> **John 14:12–14**
>
> *Verily, verily, I say unto you, He that believeth on Me, the works that I do shall he do also; and greater works than these shall he do; because I go unto My Father.*
>
> *And whatsoever ye shall ask in My Name, that will I do, that the Father may be glorified in the Son.*
>
> *If ye shall ask any thing in My Name, I will do it.*

In this passage of Scripture, Jesus is telling us how to use His Name.

John 14 is not talking about prayer. It is describing how we can speak the Word of God, in faith, expecting that Word to come to pass.

Notice in John 14, we are told to *ask* in Jesus' Name. However, in the original Greek language of the passage, the word *ask* can also be translated as *demand* or *command*. So, this passage of Scripture is not telling us to ask God to set us free; He has already done so, through Christ. What is being described here is how we are to use the Name of Jesus, standing in His authority against the devil and his works.

When Jesus ministered to the needs of others, He made declarations. He said things like: "Be healed. Come forth. Come out." He did not make requests of Satan; He gave orders—and even Creation obeyed Him. Just as Jesus declared things to be so in His earthly ministry, we can do the same, declaring by faith the miracles we are expecting to manifest.

Whatever we ask (or command) in Jesus' Name, Jesus Himself does the work. We are to do the works of Jesus as if He were here in the flesh, as He was during His earthly ministry. And we shall do *greater works* because He only had three years on Earth, operating in a small part of our world, while we have had over 2,000 years to do the miraculous works of God—preaching the Gospel with signs and wonders following—all over the Earth.

In Mark 16 as well, Jesus told us to speak the Word, to ask or demand something to be done. Christians have a right to command the things described in Luke 4 and Mark 16 to come to pass in Jesus' Name, such as commanding devils to come out.

The Name of Jesus in Prayer

There is another way that we can use the Name of Jesus—and that is in the realm of prayer. We see this in John 16.

> **John 16:23–24**
>
> *And in that day ye shall ask Me nothing. Verily, verily, I say unto you, Whatsoever ye shall ask the Father in My Name, He will give it you.*
>
> *Hitherto have ye asked nothing in My Name: ask, and ye shall receive, that your joy may be full.*

This passage is talking about what our rights would be with God the Father after Jesus' resurrection. Following the resurrection, whatever believers ask God to do in Jesus' Name, as long as it is in accordance with His will as set out in the Bible, He will do it, so that our joy will be made full. When we pray, therefore, we are to pray to God the Father in the Name of Jesus. Because Jesus sits at the Father's right hand, He's there to intercede for us, and God the Father answers our prayers.

Now, many Christians confuse how to use the Name of Jesus as described in John 14 versus what John 16 says. But the two passages of Scripture are teaching us about two different ways we can use the Name of Jesus. I want you to understand the distinction, so you will be successful in exercising your authority in Christ.

Prayer is used for the purposes of learning God's will when we don't already know it, asking for His help and empowerment to do His will when our bodies or minds don't want to do it, asking Him to provide for our needs, and interceding on behalf of others. We don't pray to God to ask Him to do something about the devil, because He's already taken care of the devil. The devil is already under our feet.

This is why, in John 14, Jesus tells us to command the devil to obey, and Jesus will enforce it. That passage is telling us how to deal with Satan. Mark 16:15–20 is doing the same thing. When you cast out a devil, you say, "In Jesus' Name, go!" You are not asking God to do something; instead, you are demanding that the demon do something.

Acts 16:16–18
And it came to pass, as we went to prayer, a certain damsel possessed with a spirit of divination met us, which brought her masters much gain by soothsaying:

The same followed Paul and us, and cried, saying, These men are the servants of the most high God, which shew unto us the way of salvation.

And this did she many days. But Paul, being grieved, turned and said to the spirit, I command thee in the Name of Jesus Christ to come out of her. And he came out the same hour.

Here, the apostle Paul commanded a demon, in Jesus' Name, to come out of a woman who was possessed. And that demon had to obey the Name of Jesus.

The Power of the Name in the Life of a Believer

Acts 3:6 (NIV)
Then Peter said, "Silver or gold I do not have, but what I do have I give you. In the Name of Jesus Christ of Nazareth, walk."

In this passage of Acts, Peter comes into contact with a lame man, who asked him for some money. Peter did what Jesus had taught Him: "Whatsoever you command, or demand, in My Name, I will do it." Peter said, "Rise and walk." The man was healed, and the religious leaders were upset. So, Peter began to talk with them.

> **Acts 3:16 (NIV)**
> *By faith in the Name of Jesus, this man whom you see and know was made strong. It is Jesus' Name and the faith that comes through Him that has completely healed him, as you can all see.*

Peter explained to the religious leaders how the man was healed. It was through faith in the Name of Jesus! We must believe the Name of Jesus is more powerful than any name in Heaven, Earth, or Hell.

Believers and the Name of Jesus

So, how does His Name relate to you and me as born-again believers?

The Bible says that if you're born again, old things are passed away and all things have become new. You are now part of the Body of Christ. This means Satan has no authority over you. In Proverbs 26:2, it says curses are like a bird that flies around, but finds no place to land because there is no cause for you to be cursed anymore. The devil himself can't put a curse on you, and the curse of the Law can't come upon you either. Because you're righteous in God's sight, it doesn't matter what anyone tries to do to you. Nothing can violate your righteousness.

In other words, you are freer than you may realize! In fact, many believers don't know how free in Jesus they are. Why is this so?

Jesus told us that anyone who continues in the Word will be His disciple, and the truth would set him free. Many believers, however, are simply ignorant of the full truth of His Word. Either they are not being taught properly in their churches, or they are not studying the Word of God to learn what it says. As a result, they believe teachings that have no basis in the Scriptures.

In many Christian circles, for example, there is a lot of teaching on generational curses, and it is wrong! I don't care if you come from fifteen generations of Satan worshippers—if you're born again, you now belong to a different family. But this is a perfect example of how the devil operates. One way Satan deceives Christians is to convince them to believe superstitions rather than God's Word, or to persuade them that he and his demons are more powerful than they really are.

The way that something from the past has a hold on a believer is if the believer either does not know (*My people are destroyed for the lack of knowledge*, Hosea 4:6), or does not believe that they are a new creation (*old things are passed away,* 2 Corinthians 5:17). They're not bringing their soul (their mind) under subjection to the Word of God.

People who talk about generational curses use the Old Testament verse where God said he would *visit the iniquity of the fathers upon the children, and upon the children's children, unto the third and to the fourth generation* (Exodus 34:7). What they fail to see is what God promised in connection with the New Covenant.

Jeremiah 31:29–31

In those days they shall say no more, The fathers have eaten a sour grape, and the children's teeth are set on edge.

But every one shall die for his own iniquity: every man that eateth the sour grape, his teeth shall be set on edge.

Behold, the days come, saith the Lord, that I will make a new covenant with the house of Israel, and with the house of Judah.

Ezekiel 18:1–4

The word of the Lord came unto me again, saying,

What mean ye, that ye use this proverb concerning the land of Israel, saying, The fathers have eaten sour grapes, and the children's teeth are set on edge?

As I live, saith the Lord God, ye shall not have occasion any more to use this proverb in Israel.

Behold, all souls are mine; as the soul of the father, so also the soul of the son is mine: the soul that sinneth, it shall die.

What these verses are saying is that each person is responsible for their own sin and cannot blame their father (or anyone else, for that matter).

The devil is a liar (John 8:44). And he tries to get believers into a state of fear, because who you fear is who you serve. Do you fear God or Satan? As believers, we are to fear God with reverence, and we don't have to be afraid of Satan.

The Name of Jesus in Action

The well-known evangelist Lester Sumrall once recalled an event in his life that illustrates this point. One time, while Sumrall was ministering in Africa, Satan caused a great wind to blow into his room and move the bed. Sumrall woke up, but he didn't become afraid, and he didn't spend a lot of time praying and rebuking the devil. He simply said, in faith, "Put it back!" And then he went back to sleep.

When he awoke the next morning, everything in his room was back in order. Why? Because Sumrall feared God rather than Satan, and he knew he could take authority over the devil, so he did. And Satan had to obey the command of a Christian who understood his authority in Christ.

This is all part of the authority of the believer. Satan is under our feet! I don't care if he shows up with twelve legions of demons in your room tonight. You can laugh in his face and cast him out, in Jesus' Name!

Here is another example of what it looks like when believers know their authority in Christ and exercise that authority in faith. One time, the preacher Smith Wigglesworth was called to come and cast demons out of a woman. As Wigglesworth walked inside the home, the demon power was in full manifestation of vile cursing. He commanded the evil spirits to come out and turned around to walk out. The woman followed behind him and began to curse him.

He turned and spoke with authority, "I told you to leave!" Then he left. The woman was completely delivered.

Can you picture this? Several men had been praying for the girl all night long, yet nothing happened. One man came in and spoke the Word of God in faith, not moved by what Satan was doing, and exercised his authority in Christ. Several Christians were bound by superstition, afraid of Satan. One believer exercised his authority—despite all the negative circumstances—and left knowing what he spoke was done, in Jesus' Name. Satan had no choice but to leave the girl.

This is exactly how you and I need to deal with Satan. Don't argue all night long with him. Don't believe he is so powerful that you can't take authority over him. Nothing is further from the truth! It doesn't take 500 people praying to get something done—it takes one believer who knows and exercises his or her authority.

There's too much superstition in the Church. Christians are bound with fear, afraid of Satan, when we are seated with Christ and need not fear the devil any longer. You and I are redeemed from all the power of the enemy.

> **Luke 10:19 (NKJV)**
> *Behold, I give you the authority to trample on serpents and scorpions, and over all the power of the enemy, and nothing shall by any means hurt you.*

When you know who you are in Christ, understanding and having faith in the fact that you are seated with Christ, with all things under your feet, then you will not be moved by the attacks of the enemy. You and I belong to the generation of Jesus Christ, a spiritual race called the Church. We are victorious over the devil, through Christ.

Renew Your Mind to Understand Your Authority

So, why do so many Christians believe superstitions or fall victim to the lies of the devil? It is because we have a soul—our mind, will, and emotions—and most of us have trained that soul in all the ways of the world for years before we became born again. While we are new creations, our minds must be renewed daily with the Word of God so we can think like Christ and believe the truth, not lies. We have to make our bodies and minds servants to our spirits, and not masters.

You have been crucified with Christ. The old "you" is dead. So, don't try to fix something that's dead. Forget the idea of generational curses. Forget the past. Live in the now, in your new life in Christ, because there's liberty in this newness of life that you have in Him.

The foolish, man-made doctrines and beliefs that cause some to look for and fear demons everywhere is ultimately tied to the fleshly, carnal, and worldly behavior. It is not based on what Jesus wrought for us on the Cross, and through His Resurrection. Most of the time, the struggles we face in life are the direct result of sinning, or failing to follow God's direction.

> **Colossians 2:13–15**
>
> *And you, being dead in your sins and the uncircumcision of your flesh, hath He quickened together with Him, having forgiven you all trespasses;*
>
> *Blotting out the handwriting of ordinances that was against us, which was contrary to us, and took it out of the way, nailing it to His Cross;*
>
> *And having spoiled principalities and powers, He made a shew of them openly, triumphing over them in it.*

Again, we do not need to ever fear the devil, because we are more than conquerors through Him who loves us. We have actually become one with Jesus, and we share in His victory. This means we share in His authority too.

The Name of Jesus works for you too—just as it did for Peter, Paul, the disciples, Lester Sumrall, and Smith Wigglesworth! Whenever a believer commands devils to go or sickness to leave, it must happen. Stand strong in faith! Faith in the Name of Jesus changes situations. There's nothing that can stand against His Name!

CHAPTER 9

THE PRESENT-DAY MINISTRY OF JESUS

Why is the blood of Jesus a weapon to overcome the devil? It's because, through the shed blood of Jesus, we are made righteous in God's sight, and therefore there's no sin that the devil can use to come against us with.

The blood of Jesus has paid the price for sin; and it is no longer sin that separates us from God. Rather, it is our choice to accept the payment for that sin, through Jesus, that brings us near to Him.

> **Romans 5:17**
> *For if by one man's offence death reigned by one; much more they which receive abundance of grace and of the gift of righteousness shall reign in life by one, Jesus Christ.*

Christians are made righteous by our faith in the blood of Jesus, trusting in what He has accomplished for us, and believing in Him as Lord and Savior. When Satan, known as the accuser, comes against you with accusations, it's the blood of Jesus that silences him.

We have received the gift of righteousness by faith in His blood to cleanse us and make us right with God. And it's our faith in Him and His shed blood that forms the foundation of His present-day ministry through us, His Church. We can see this foundation clearly, not just in the New Testament, but in the Old Testament as well. It is evident in how the very temple at Jerusalem was crafted.

> **Romans 3:25**
> *Whom God hath set forth to be a propitiation through faith in His blood, to declare His righteousness for the remission of sins that are past, through the forbearance of God.*

The word *propitiation* in the original Greek language of this verse means "Mercy Seat." So, you could also read the verse this way: *Whom God hath set forth to be our Mercy Seat through faith in His blood...*

Jesus has become our Mercy Seat through faith in His blood. But what is the Mercy Seat, and why is it meaningful to Christians today?

Meeting with God

In the Jewish temple, where the priests worshipped God and offered sacrifices to cover the sins of their people, various rituals took place to commemorate various elements of our relationship with God. Every element of these acts of worship were set forth by God Himself, as signs of what would one day come when He sent His Son, Jesus Christ.

One of the most significant of these activities happened each year on the Day of Atonement, which is how the Mercy Seat and the Ark of the Covenant gain relevance to us today.

> **Exodus 25:21–22 (NKJV)**
> *You shall put the mercy seat on top of the ark, and in the ark you shall put the Testimony that I will give you.*

And there I will meet with you, and I will speak with you from above the mercy seat, from between the two cherubim which are on the ark of the Testimony, about everything which I will give you in commandment to the children of Israel.

Notice that the Mercy Seat is a part of the Ark of the Covenant. It is set into the top of the Ark, between two angels (or cherubim)—symbolic of God's throne in Heaven, where He dwells in all His majesty and glory. Within the Ark were placed the stone tablets that held the Law God gave Moses—symbolic of the Word of God. The Ark represents God's power, His perfection, and His holiness. It was kept in a set-apart place in the Temple called the Holy of Holies, where only the High Priest was permitted to enter, and only once a year on the Day of Atonement.

In many ways, the Ark and the Holy of Holies make it clear that God is set apart from all that is unholy and profane. And after the fall of Adam and Eve, humans became tainted by sin.

Yet God makes it clear in Exodus that He wishes to meet with His people. And where will He meet with us? At the Mercy Seat. This is significant because we know that through our own works, we can never be righteous or holy enough to enter God's presence. Instead, He must extend His mercy to us, allowing us into His presence of His own choice. In the Old Testament days, before Jesus came, sin was covered by the shedding of the blood of animals.

The holiest of these offerings were made on the Day of Atonement, also known today as Yom Kippur. On this day, the High Priest would perform several offerings and actions, including the sending of a goat out into the wilderness, representing the sins of the people, and the sacrifice of a bull, whose blood was placed on the Ark of the Covenant, including the Mercy Seat.

When God accepted these sacrifices, the High Priest would exit the Holy of Holies, unharmed. It was a sign that God was pleased with the offerings.

Thus, on the Day of Atonement, the Israelites knew their sins were forgiven for the year. However, they had to repeat the sacrifice every year, because the payment for their sins at the time was mere animal blood. This animal blood was a symbol of what was to come—the only blood that can eternally save us—the blood of Jesus, our Savior. But because Jesus had not yet come, the people of Israel could use the animal blood as a temporary covering, putting their faith in God to have mercy on them and one day pay the price for them in full.

But today, Romans 3:25 says Jesus became our Mercy Seat through faith in His blood. When God looks at the blood of Jesus, He doesn't see the Law that condemns—He sees what Jesus accomplished through His death, burial, resurrection, and ascension.

As we have already discussed in an earlier chapter, Satan knows that Christians are not perfect, so he accuses us before God. Revelation 12, however, says we have overcome his accusations by the blood of the Lamb, Jesus, who was offered up for our sins for all time.

> **Hebrews 2:17 (NKJV)**
> *Therefore, in all things He had to be made like His brethren, that He might be a merciful and faithful High Priest in things pertaining to God, to make propitiation for the sins of the people.*

Like the High Priests of the Old Testament, Jesus entered into the true Holy of Holies in Heaven, using His own shed blood as the atoning sacrifice after His resurrection. He placed His own blood on the

Mercy Seat of Heaven. God accepted this offering as full, eternal payment for our sins. Now, for everyone who believes in Jesus and becomes a part of His Body, by faith, there is eternal forgiveness of sin. For us as believers, there is no need for further blood sacrifices. The blood of Jesus has paid for it all.

So, let's summarize. Jesus overcame the devil and sits at the right hand of the Father. The devil and all his demons are under His feet, which means they're under our feet. All authority in Heaven and in Earth is given to Jesus. He has the Name above every name, and He gave us His authority to preach the Word and go forth in His Name, heal the sick, cast out devils, preach the Gospel, and do the works that He did.

To do this work, He has given us weapons that are mighty through God—powerful weapons to use against our spiritual foe, the devil, and evils like sickness, lack, and oppression. Our chief weapons are the sword of the Spirit, which is the Word of God; the Name of Jesus; the blood of Jesus; and our faith in Him.

The Blood Speaks

Hebrews 12:22–24 (NKJV)

But you have come to Mount Zion and to the city of the living God, the heavenly Jerusalem, to an innumerable company of angels,

To the general assembly and church of the firstborn who are registered in Heaven, to God the Judge of all, to the spirits of just men made perfect,

To Jesus the Mediator of the new covenant, and to the blood of sprinkling that speaks better things than that of Abel.

IN MY NAME

The blood of Jesus, interestingly enough, is not silent. It has a voice. It speaks. In fact, this passage in Hebrews tells us that the blood of Jesus speaks better things than Abel's blood. Let's look at what this means.

In the Book of Genesis, after Adam and Eve are forced to leave the Garden of Eden due to sin, they have children, including two sons named Cain and Abel. One day, both of these young men offered sacrifices to God. But while Abel offered his best lamb as an offering of blood, Cain only offered some meager fruits and vegetables, and he made his offering half-heartedly.

God accepted Abel's sacrifice but not Cain's. And Cain grew jealous and angry. He killed his brother Abel. When God came to confront Cain about the evil he had done, Cain denied he had done anything. God said, "I hear the voice of your brother's blood calling to me from the ground." Abel's blood cried out to God for justice, for vengeance against Cain's sin.

But Jesus' blood cries out to God for something better. His blood is speaking something in Heaven right now.

> **1 John 5:8 (NKJV)**
> *And there are three that bear witness on earth: the Spirit, the water, and the blood; and these three agree as one.*

What is the blood saying on our behalf?

> **Romans 5:8–10 (NKJV)**
> *But God demonstrates His own love toward us, in that while we were still sinners, Christ died for us.*

Much more then, having now been justified by His blood, we shall be saved from wrath through Him.

For if when we were enemies we were reconciled to God through the death of His Son, much more, having been reconciled, we shall be saved by His life.

Jesus Cut a New Covenant

On the day that Jesus shed His blood and died on the Cross, something miraculous happened in the Temple at Jerusalem. The veil that separated the people from the Holy of Holies was split in two. The separation was ended through the shed blood of Jesus. The old way of making animal sacrifices was rendered unnecessary. From that moment forward, a new way of relating to God became possible—a relationship with Him through His Son, Jesus. This ushered in what we call the New Covenant.

It is this New Covenant that the Church, the Body of Christ, operates under today. Everything that we are called to do today as believers, everything that we have authority to do in His Name, is part of this New Covenant we have through God the Father through Jesus.

Jesus paid for our sins through His shed blood and gave us authority on the Earth in His Name. This is His part of the covenant with us. Our part is to be faithful to Him and to carry out His works in the Earth. The present-day ministry of Jesus happens through the Body of Christ because of this New Covenant, which we entered into when we accepted Him as Lord and Savior.

The blood of Jesus plainly, unreservedly declares that we are forgiven of our sin and made righteous in His sight. It declares boldly the truth of John 3:16—that whosoever believes in Him will be saved. It declares without a doubt that when His Body, His Church, speaks His Word in faith or prays in His name, all things in Heaven, on Earth, and under the Earth are to obey.

This is the present-day ministry of Jesus. It is Him at work in us and through us to do all that He would do if He were here in the flesh. Through us, He is present and at work in the Earth, ready to change lives, to save, heal, deliver, and restore.

The only question that remains today is not what God will do for us. He has done it all already, in Christ. The question is, what will we do for Him? Will we allow Him to work through us? Will we learn to exercise His authority in the Earth? The next section of this book discusses exactly how we, as His Body, can do so.

SECTION 3:

Practical Application: How to Use His Authority

CHAPTER 10

HOW DO I USE AUTHORITY?

There are three reasons Satan is still at work in the Earth: First, individuals must receive what Jesus did on the Cross through faith. If they don't, Satan can work through them. Since there are wicked people on Earth, Satan has lots of opportunities to work in the Earth. Second, Satan uses lies to deceive others into believing him. If he is successful at this deception, he can manifest himself in the Earth. Third, the Church, the Body of Christ, is not taking its authority—the authority that Jesus gave us when He arose from the dead.

In all three cases, there is a sure way to use our authority and counter the work of the devil in the Earth: the preaching, teaching, and declaring of God's Word. Why is this so? Let's take a closer look at several Scriptures that illustrate the power of God's Word over the devil.

Romans 10:14–17 (NKJV)
How then shall they call on Him in whom they have not believed? And how shall they believe in Him of whom they have not heard? And how shall they hear without a preacher?

And how shall they preach unless they are sent? As it is written: "How beautiful are the feet of those who preach the Gospel of peace, who bring glad tidings of good things!"

But they have not all obeyed the Gospel. For Isaiah says, "Lord, who has believed our report?"

IN MY NAME

So then faith comes by hearing, and hearing by the Word of God.

This Scripture is probably one you are very familiar with, and it is foundational to how we use our faith. Romans tells us that faith comes as we hear God's Word—and not just hear it with our ears. We must hear it and take it into our heart, into our inner man, where it can give birth to faith and confidence in God. As God's Word becomes alive to us, it produces faith, and we can use that faith to receive God's promises and resist the works of the devil.

John 8:31–32 (NKJV)

Then Jesus said to those Jews who believed Him, "If you abide in My Word, you are My disciples indeed.

And you shall know the truth, and the truth shall make you free."

Not only does God's Word build faith in us, but it also reveals the truth to us. Remember that the devil works through deception. He is a liar who depends on our believing his lies so he can control us. When we know the truth, those lies will be exposed for what they are. And when we know the truth—that in Christ, the Church is seated in heavenly places, with authority over the devil—then Satan can't manipulate us or keep us bound.

Psalm 119:130 (NKJV)

The entrance of Your words gives light; it gives understanding to the simple.

This verse depicts how the Word of God helps us to know the

truth—it brings light into the darkness and ignorance that Satan wants the world to operate in. Other people may not have light on a matter, but those of us who are in the Body of Christ can rely on God's Word to illuminate our situation and bring us spiritual understanding.

Now, what do you do if you meet with unbelief as you are sharing God's Word? Follow the example of Jesus in the Gospel of Mark.

> **Mark 6:4–6 (NKJV)**
>
> *But Jesus said to them, "A prophet is not without honor except in his own country, among his own relatives, and in his own house."*
>
> *Now He could do no mighty work there, except that He laid His hands on a few sick people and healed them.*
>
> *And He marveled because of their unbelief. Then He went about the villages in a circuit, teaching.*

When Jesus ran into unbelief and was unable to perform any miracles, He immediately went into the synagogues to teach. The teaching and preaching of the Word of God changes the spiritual atmosphere of a place and allows God to move. As the Gospel is preached, people can begin to respond to it with faith, and thus territory is gained for the Kingdom of God. Remember, the Kingdom of God expands every time someone is saved, healed, delivered or restored.

Why is this fact significant? It's because the authority of the Body of Christ expands as God's Kingdom expands. More people and more cities come under the authority of Christ as people submit to Him.

> **2 Corinthians 10:3–5**
>
> *For though we walk in the flesh, we do not war after the flesh:*
>
> *(For the weapons of our warfare are not carnal, but mighty through God to the pulling down of strong holds;)*
>
> *Casting down imaginations, and every high thing that exalteth itself against the knowledge of God, and bringing into captivity every thought to the obedience of Christ;*

The devil blinds the minds of unbelievers so that he can control them. The preaching of the Gospel is the only thing that brings freedom. As we share the truth of what Jesus has done, the ability to believe God is birthed in those who hear it. This allows a man or woman to accept or reject Jesus based on the truth of the Gospel. The primary weapon of our warfare is the preaching of God's Word, which is why Paul makes a bold statement in Romans 1:16.

> **Romans 1:16**
>
> *For I am not ashamed of the Gospel of Christ: for it is the power of God unto salvation to every one that believeth...*

The Power of God's Word

> **Ephesians 6:11–18**
>
> *Put on the whole armour of God, that ye may be able to stand against the wiles of the devil.*
>
> *For we wrestle not against flesh and blood, but against principalities, against powers, against the rulers of the darkness of this world, against spiritual wickedness in high places.*
>
> *Wherefore take unto you the whole armour of God, that ye may be able to withstand in the evil day, and having done all, to stand.*

HOW DO I USE AUTHORITY?

Stand therefore, having your loins girt about with truth, and having on the breastplate of righteousness;

And your feet shod with the preparation of the Gospel of peace;

Above all, taking the shield of faith, wherewith ye shall be able to quench all the fiery darts of the wicked.

And take the helmet of salvation, and the sword of the Spirit, which is the Word of God:

Praying always with all prayer and supplication in the Spirit, and watching thereunto with all perseverance and supplication for all saints.

In this well-known passage of Scripture, we are told by the apostle Paul to put on the armor of God daily. The pieces of armor are meant to protect us from the enemy. Notice in this list, there is only one weapon: the sword of the spirit, the Word of God. When we preach the truth, the truth will come against the lies of Satan that blind the unbeliever. And the Word of God also comes against the deceptions he tries to use against us, the Body of Christ. The primary way Christians come against Satan is by preaching the truth of the Gospel.

Two Realms of God-given Authority

The biggest question Christians must answer is how to use the authority given to us by God. So, let us consider what God-given authority looks like and how it functions. There are two main forms that God-given authority can take in the Earth: natural authority and spiritual authority.

Romans 13:1–4

Let every soul be subject unto the higher powers. For there is no power but of God: the powers that be are ordained of God.

Whosoever therefore resisteth the power, resisteth the ordinance of God: and they that resist shall receive to themselves damnation.

For rulers are not a terror to good works, but to the evil. Wilt thou then not be afraid of the power? do that which is good, and thou shalt have praise of the same:

For he is the minister of God to thee for good. But if thou do that which is evil, be afraid; for he beareth not the sword in vain: for he is the minister of God, a revenger to execute wrath upon him that doeth evil.

In this passage of Scripture, Paul discusses the natural authorities in the Earth, such as the police and governments. These institutions are given to us by God to help keep order in the natural realm, as we go about our daily lives. Paul tells us to respect these natural authorities and obey the laws of the land, even though these authorities are not perfect.

1 Peter 2:13–16

Submit yourselves to every ordinance of man for the Lord's sake: whether it be to the king, as supreme;

Or unto governors, as unto them that are sent by him for the punishment of evildoers, and for the praise of them that do well.

For so is the will of God, that with well doing ye may put to silence the ignorance of foolish men:

As free, and not using your liberty for a cloke of maliciousness, but as the servants of God.

This passage also tells Christians to respect and obey natural authorities. In general, unless we are being asked to violate God's Word, Christians are to obey the law of the land. Even our protests should be peaceful.

Why must Christians obey these natural laws and respect our leaders and the existing natural authorities? In part, we are doing so to help promote God's will in the Earth.

> **1 Timothy 2:1–4**
> *I exhort therefore, that, first of all, supplications, prayers, intercessions, and giving of thanks, be made for all men;*
>
> *For kings, and for all that are in authority; that we may lead a quiet and peaceable life in all godliness and honesty.*
>
> *For this is good and acceptable in the sight of God our Saviour;*
>
> *Who will have all men to be saved, and to come unto the knowledge of the truth.*

God established authority in the Earth because there would be chaos and anarchy without it. Unsaved people don't always pursue God's will, after all, and sadly, many would do great harm if not for the threat of punishment they would incur for doing evil. Some form of law is always needed to keep evil-doing in check.

Of course, natural authorities are not perfect—no one is perfect—and many are corrupt. Nonetheless, natural authorities still serve the purpose of keeping order. For this reason, Christians are to respect natural authorities except when the will of God as stated in His Word is being directly violated, and we as Christians are being forced to make a choice between man and God.

An example of this can be seen in the book of Daniel, where the three young Hebrew men were commanded to bow to the idol of Nebuchadnezzar, exalting this human king over God. In this, the Hebrews were right to disobey—it was a matter of embracing or denying God. Note that the men were ready to suffer the punishment the king had ordered—death by fire. They did not try to flee, but accepted their death sentence. God chose to do a miracle and deliver them.

In other instances, even when we might not always like the law, if it doesn't ask us to directly deny God or disobey Him, we must accept and obey man's law. Taxes are never popular, and the Romans weren't popular with the nations that they conquered, including Israel. But the tax law did not require people to deny God; it just required them to pay their taxes and obey the natural authorities set in place.

Another aspect to consider is that God has established both natural authorities and spiritual authorities, which indicates that He values both. As the following verse reveals, God views those who have authority as guardians who watch over our souls and help to protect us from harm.

> **Hebrews 13:17**
> *Obey them that have the rule over you, and submit yourselves: for they watch for your souls, as they that must give account, that they may do it with joy, and not with grief: for that is unprofitable for you.*

How to Use Your Authority in Christ

What are we—the Church, the Body of Christ—supposed to do with the spiritual authority Jesus has given us?

2 Corinthians 4:3–4 (NKJV)

But even if our Gospel is veiled, it is veiled to those who are perishing,

Whose minds the god of this age has blinded, who do not believe, lest the light of the Gospel of the glory of Christ, who is the image of God, should shine on them.

Let me reiterate this important truth about the Church and the devil: The only authority the devil has in the Earth now is the authority that people give him. He rules only in the hearts of people who are in unbelief and who refuse to believe the truth of God's Word. Christians, though, know the truth and are set free.

Not only do we as Christians know the truth, but we also know the devil has no authority over us. The only reason there is evil in the world today is that there are men and women who have not been born again, and they allow Satan to use them.

How are Christians supposed to deal with Satan? First Peter makes the answer clear.

1 Peter 5:8–9 (NKJV)

Be sober, be vigilant; because your adversary the devil walks about like a roaring lion, seeking whom he may devour.

Resist him, steadfast in the faith, knowing that the same sufferings are experienced by your brotherhood in the world.

Satan is our adversary, our enemy, and the Scripture passage above compares him to a lion roaming around restlessly, hunting for prey. Lions target the weakest animal in the herd—the one that will be the easiest to bring down, kill, and eat. Satan is the same way. He is looking for those who will easily be brought down by his lies and attacks.

But notice that Satan cannot simply devour everyone he sees. He can only devour those who are vulnerable to him, just as a lion can't devour an entire herd of gazelles, just the one that is sickly or young enough for it to catch. Satan can only blind the eyes of those who don't believe God's Word and don't know the truth. He's looking for people to control through unbelief or ignorance.

> **James 4:7 (NKJV)**
> *Therefore submit to God. Resist the devil and he will flee from you.*

Both Peter and James make it clear how to respond to the devil. We are to submit to God, stand steadfast in our faith in Him, and resist the devil's lies and attacks with the truth and power of God's Word. What happens when we do this? The Bible is clear about this as well—the devil will flee. The devil will run away from the Body of Christ as we act on our authority over him, because he has to. Because of what Christ accomplished through the Cross, the devil *must* obey us and submit to the authority of God that we are exercising. He has no choice about it.

> **James 2:19 (NKJV)**
> *You believe that there is one God. You do well. Even the demons believe—and tremble!*

This passage clearly states that the devil and his demon cohorts tremble in fear because they know what Jesus did to them at the Cross. They know what sentence Jesus rendered against them at His resurrection. Jesus defeated them utterly. It's only when Christians are ignorant of what God has achieved for us in Christ that Satan has any power.

Ephesians 4:27 (NKJV)
...nor give place to the devil.

Christians are instructed to not give Satan any room in their lives. Yet with all the authority Jesus has given to the Church, it is amazing how miserably Christians have often failed to exercise that authority. However, throughout the ages, there have been groups of Christians who discovered their authority in Christ and learned to successfully walk it out, bringing about great miracles, salvations, and God's Kingdom manifested in the Earth. Brother Kenneth E. Hagin, who began Rhema Bible Training College, is one of the men God raised up in times past and commissioned to go teach God's people faith. This commissioning was and is a part of preparing Christians to usher in the end-times and the Second Coming of Jesus Christ.

As you consider the believer's authority today, don't get discouraged by the evils that you see happening in the world. When it looks like Satan is having his way, it does not mean that Jesus' victory is incomplete. Rather, it indicates that the Church has failed to exercise its authority. As we come to understand Satan's defeat at the Cross and the power of the blood of Jesus, we can also come to understand our own authority in Him and use it to impact our world. As Kenneth E. Hagin put it in his book, *The Believer's Authority*:

> Satan has succeeded in keeping God's people blind to what happened to him at the Cross. By deceiving, he has convinced the

IN MY NAME

> Church that he is almost as powerful as God when in truth, he has no power at all. He has no legal standing, no rights, no authority. He knows that when the church finally realizes his defeat and how to use their authority, he will be finished.[4]

Satan was finished at the Cross and the Resurrection over 2,000 years ago. This is why he hopes God's people will remain ignorant of his defeat, ignorant of our power, and unaware of how to use our authority over him.

Christians who study and learn how to use their authority are Satan's biggest headache. Once you know how to use your authority over him, he will try to stop you through discouragement or causing you to lose faith and hope. This is why resisting Satan until he flees from you is crucial. Give him no place in your life. Let's add a few more truths to your arsenal.

Ephesians 6:10–11 (NIV)
Finally, be strong in the Lord and in His mighty power.

Put on the full armor of God, so that you can take your stand against the devil's schemes.

Notice that the first thing God tells us in this passage about the armor of God is that we are to *be strong in the Lord*. That's not a suggestion; it's an order. We are to be strong in the Lord, because we're already victorious through Him. Once we know this, we are to put on the armor of God.

---
[4] Hagin, K.E. (1985). The believer's authority. Broken Arrow, OK: Faith Library Publications.

Ephesians 6:12 (NIV)

For our struggle is not against flesh and blood, but against the rulers, against the authorities, against the powers of this dark world and against the spiritual forces of evil in the heavenly realms.

There is still evil in the world. Satan still deceives people and uses them to do wicked things and cause harm in our world. But we already know what to do about it.

Ephesians 6:13–15 (NIV)

Therefore put on the full armor of God, so that when the day of evil comes, you may be able to stand your ground, and after you have done everything, to stand.

Stand firm then, with the belt of truth buckled around your waist, with the breastplate of righteousness in place,

And with your feet fitted with the readiness that comes from the Gospel of peace.

According to God's Word, we can stand and resist the enemy. The armor of God is given to us so we can stand in the midst of any circumstance and win! One way to use our authority is to draw on what God has given us, as depicted by the armor of God described in Ephesians 6.

Consider the belt of truth in verse 14. When you read the word *loins*, think of the upper leg and abdominal muscles. They're the core of our body—and the core of our human strength. Verse 14 says God clothes our loins with truth. The truth, the Word of God, is what brings us the greatest strength in life. In the days of Paul, soldiers wore breastplates to protect their hearts, their most vital organ. Likewise, Christians are told to put on the breastplate of righteousness. Our hearts need to be protected against any attacks that challenge our right standing with God.

How are we saved? According to Romans 10:10, we believe in our heart that Jesus was raised from the dead and we confess Him as Lord. This is believing in our heart *unto righteousness*. By believing in Jesus' victory over Satan when He was raised from the dead, Christians stand against Satan's attacks on their right standing with God. Christ declared us righteous when He was resurrected. Trusting in the power of His resurrection will protect our hearts from discouragement in the midst of any attack.

The next verse instructs us to have our feet shod with the Gospel of peace. Why your feet? Because they take you places. Our feet carry us where we need to go as we follow God's will for our lives. Our feet represent what we do daily for the Lord. The Christian walk is characterized by our actions. Walking in the Gospel of peace means knowing God has forgiven us. And because we know we have peace with God through Christ, we share that good news with others, so they can have that peace too. The Bible says blessed are the feet of those who share the Gospel, so it's important to share it—and our testimony—with others.

> **Ephesians 6:16–18 (NIV)**
> *In addition to all this, take up the shield of faith, with which you can extinguish all the flaming arrows of the evil one.*
>
> *Take the helmet of salvation and the sword of the Spirit, which is the Word of God.*
>
> *And pray in the Spirit on all occasions with all kinds of prayers and requests. With this in mind, be alert and always keep on praying for all the Lord's people.*

In the King James Version of verse 16, it says we are to take up the shield of faith *above all else*. Why is this so important? Because the shield of faith puts out the fiery darts Satan throws our way. Faith is the way that we *resist* him.

What are these *fiery darts*? They are the attacks that the devil tries to make us succumb to. These are issues and situations that God has set us free from, things we have authority over, if we will exercise that authority.

When sickness, for example, tries to come against us, it is an attack of the devil, for we have been healed through Christ (1 Peter 2:24). So, how do we extinguish that dart? We exercise faith in the healing Jesus has won for us. When other attacks come against us—whether it is poverty, lack, sorrow, anger, unforgiveness, or some other evil thing—those fiery darts of the devil can be extinguished as we shield ourselves with faith, trusting in God's Word to give us joy, comfort us, provide for us, restore us, and vindicate us.

What does the helmet of salvation protect? The mind. In other words, wearing the helmet of salvation means that we are renewing our mind to what the Bible says about us. Meditating on what Jesus did for us protects us from fear and doubt. Even if we don't understand why something is happening, we can protect our mind from discouragement and unbelief by meditating on the salvation of God and His faithfulness to keep His Word to us.

The last piece of armor mentioned in Ephesians 6 is the sword of the Spirit, which is the Word of God. Every other piece of armor acts as a defensive element to protect us. The sword of the Spirit is the only offensive tool because God's Word is the tool we are to use to fight back when the devil attacks.

How did Jesus use the Word of God? When Satan said to Jesus, "If you're the Son of God, do this," Jesus replied, "It is written." Jesus' response to all of Satan's attacks in the wilderness was to counter the devil with the truth of God's Word. The sword of the Spirit—God's Word—cuts down Satan's attack.

> **Hebrews 4:12 (NIV)**
>
> *For the Word of God is alive and active. Sharper than any double-edged sword, it penetrates even to dividing soul and spirit, joints and marrow; it judges the thoughts and attitudes of the heart.*

We use the Word of God as a weapon because it is living and productive. The truth in God's Word cuts through the lies and deceptions that Satan puts forth. No matter what a situation may look like, God's Word reveals the truth and makes our path clear. We must keep the Word of God in our hearts and minds, and then speak it out of our mouths in faith whenever a situation comes against us. Speaking Scriptures in faith over a situation is what changes it for our good.

> **2 Corinthians 2:14–15 (NIV)**
>
> *But thanks be to God, who always leads us as captives in Christ's triumphal procession and uses us to spread the aroma of the knowledge of Him everywhere.*
>
> *For we are to God the pleasing aroma of Christ among those who are being saved and those who are perishing.*

How often do Christians win? Always!

2 Corinthians 10:4–5 (NIV)

The weapons we fight with are not the weapons of the world. On the contrary, they have divine power to demolish strongholds.

We demolish arguments and every pretension that sets itself up against the knowledge of God, and we take captive every thought to make it obedient to Christ.

Our weapons are mighty through God. He always causes us to triumph!

Romans 8:37 (NIV)

No, in all these things we are more than conquerors through Him who loved us.

Because we are in Christ, God has made us more than conquerors. What does it mean to be *more than a conqueror*? Here's an illustration to explain:

A man works in the fields to earn a living, sweating and shedding blood because of the hard work. His boss pays him at the end of each day; the money represents his blood, sweat, and tears. His wages mark him as a conqueror. The man goes home each night and gives his wages to his wife and family, so that they can benefit from what he has earned. His family members are more than conquerors because they did not have to work all day in the fields, yet they are enjoying the benefits of the work that was done on their behalf.

Jesus did all the work of redeeming us from sin and conquering the devil, and He gave us all the benefits. We're more than conquerors!

CHAPTER 11

SUBMISSION AND AUTHORITY

Now you know that, as Christians, we have great authority in Christ. But how do we use this authority to make an impact in our world?

Ultimately, all human and spiritual authority is rooted and grounded in God Himself, who is the Source of all the authority in the universe. So, in order to operate in the spiritual authority that Christ has given the Church, we need to understand how God has created authority to function, as well as our relationship to that authority. Let's look at how God has structured authority in the natural and spiritual realms.

First, let's consider authority in the natural realm and how it functions.

Natural Authority

I heard a minister say, "You can't get over what God has put under you, until you get under what God has put over you." This truth can be seen in the following passage.

> **Romans 13:1–4 (NKJV)**
> *Let every soul be subject to the governing authorities. For there is no authority except from God, and the authorities that exist are appointed by God.*
>
> *Therefore whoever resists the authority resists the ordinance of God, and those who*

resist will bring judgment on themselves.

For rulers are not a terror to good works, but to evil. Do you want to be unafraid of the authority? Do what is good, and you will have praise from the same.

For he is God's minister to you for good. But if you do evil, be afraid; for he does not bear the sword in vain; for he is God's minister, an avenger to execute wrath on him who practices evil.

In this passage, the Apostle Paul explains that there is no authority but what God has ordained. Why does God ordain authority in the natural realm? What is its purpose? We find the answer in First Peter.

1 Peter 2:13-14 (NKJV)
Therefore submit yourselves to every ordinance of man for the Lord's sake, whether to the king as supreme,

Or to governors, as to those who are sent by him for the punishment of evildoers and for the praise of those who do good.

God has ordained positions of authority in this earth because otherwise there would be total chaos and anarchy. A world with no rules would lead to total confusion, as people would simply do whatever they wanted to do. This is the nature of the carnal, unredeemed person—to please themselves and be self-focused. A world without a governing authority would be a world in which evil reigns unchecked. So, God ordains authority to limit evil.

Of course, the fact that God has instituted the principle of authority in the Earth doesn't mean that every man or woman in a leadership role is going to behave in a manner that honors God. There certainly have been wicked kings and rulers throughout the ages. Nonetheless, God has ordained the structure of authority to keep order in the Earth.

> **Hebrews 13:17 (NKJV)**
> *Obey those who rule over you, and be submissive, for they watch out for your souls, as those who must give account. Let them do so with joy and not with grief, for that would be unprofitable for you.*

The reason we can enjoy a relatively peaceful existence is that most people are submitting themselves to the earthly authorities that God has ordained.

Spiritual Authority

God has not only created the structure for natural, earthly authority, but He has ordained spiritual leadership in the Body of Christ as well. Just as earthly authorities keep order in the world, spiritual leadership keeps order in the Church. In order for believers to exercise their spiritual authority, they first need to understand how spiritual authority in the Church works—and be submitted to it, which is essentially submitting to God.

A Christian who rebels against spiritual leadership, refusing to take orders and submit to the authorities that God has set in place in the Body of Christ, will not be able to exercise authority in their own lives. Why? It's because they are in violation of God's principles of authority.

This is why it's important to submit to leadership with a good attitude. Whether or not you agree with the leaders doesn't matter. For instance, your job in the natural realm is to submit to your employer and do the work you were hired to do. The same principle applies to any church or ministry you serve in. Has God called you to serve Him in that church or ministry? If so, then respect the authorities there.

When most Christians think of the authority of the believer, they think about casting out devils, healing the sick, and raising the dead. However, we also operate in the power and authority of God every time we graciously submit to our spiritual leaders. Through submission, we learn to respect others and act in wisdom. God can then honor us and use us to exercise His authority in the world. We can't work alone, rebelliously, without being connected to the rest of the Body of Christ, yet expect God to use us. Working in unity with the Body of Christ is critical to our own spiritual growth.

Submitting to Authority Begins in Our Personal Lives

It is so important for Christians to understand how God looks at authority, because it's easy to talk about casting out devils, healing the sick, and raising the dead without ever understanding the bigger picture of how God intends His Kingdom to work. If you can't exercise authority in your personal lives, how do you expect to exercise authority in a ministry role?

Every one of us has been given authority over something. First of all, we all have authority over ourselves and our own personal lives. We are to live a disciplined life, willingly submitting our bodies and minds to God's Word.

The realm of our authority grows greater in marriage. Wives are to honor and respect their husbands, and husbands are to love their wives. Once children enter the picture, they are to submit to the leadership of the parents. And we as parents can guard our children by praying in faith and authority over them. We have the authority to resist the devil and keep him out of our homes and away from our families. We have the authority to believe God for healing for ourselves and our household, and to appropriate all the promises of God. This right is given to every believer.

The same is true for the business world. Business owners have authority over their business and their employees. We have a right to kick the devil out of our place of business. If we are working for someone else but have been given a position of authority, then we may exercise that role in the name of Jesus. We can pray for those we manage, pray for our department, and pray the blessings of God on the entire company.

Submission to Authority in Ministry

Beyond our own lives, we are also to submit to authority as God has created that authority in the Church. We are to respect the spiritual leadership of the local church we attend. And even spiritual leaders are to submit to their leaders and to Christ.

1 Corinthians 9:1–2 (NKJV)

Am I not an apostle? Am I not free? Have I not seen Jesus Christ our Lord? Are you not my work in the Lord?

If I am not an apostle to others, yet doubtless I am to you. For you are the seal of my apostleship in the Lord.

In the above passage of scripture, Paul is discussing his ministerial authority. And it is clear that even Paul, the great apostle, wasn't above submission. In fact, his position as a leader meant that he had to submit himself to the call of God to be a godly leader. He had to fulfill his calling as God would have him do. He had to serve well the people he had been called to minister to.

This scripture also shows us that Paul was not an apostle over everyone, but only those he had invested into and discipled. He was also recognized as an apostle by his fellow apostles and peers in ministry.

> **2 Corinthians 10:13–16 (NKJV)**
>
> *We, however, will not boast beyond measure, but within the limits of the sphere which God appointed us — a sphere which especially includes you.*
>
> *For we are not overextending ourselves (as though our authority did not extend to you), for it was to you that we came with the Gospel of Christ;*
>
> *Not boasting of things beyond measure, that is, in other men's labors, but having hope, that as your faith is increased, we shall be greatly enlarged by you in our sphere,*
>
> *To preach the Gospel in the regions beyond you, and not to boast in another man's sphere of accomplishment.*

Here, we see that as Paul's ministry expanded into other areas, so did his realm of authority. His authority depended on his submission to God to fulfill His calling. And we are to respect the authority of our fellow believers. In Paul's case, he says he came to the Corinthians humbly, to share God's Word. He did not come in an effort to steal the fruit of someone else's ministry efforts. This is why Paul wanted to travel to regions farther away, where no one had yet ministered the Word of God. He did not want to usurp another church leader's spiritual authority, which is ultimately a form of rebellion against God.

Too many times in many local churches, a minister that no one knows will show up and claim, "I'm an apostle, and God told me to come here and preach to your church." This sort of behavior is not of God because outside ministers have no authority within a local church, unless the existing leaders give them permission to minister to their congregants. The existing leaders of a local church, as they are led by God, are to be the ones who decide to invite guests to speak. Otherwise, the outside ministers have no authority there. Operating outside of God's structures of authority in this way will only bring rebellion and confusion.

Our Authority Doesn't Extend to Controlling Other People

The one thing we don't have authority over is other people's lives—unless they have willingly given us that kind of authority. While we have authority over demons and devils, we can't exercise authority over people without their consent.

People have a free will and the right to make choices for themselves. God respects the individual's free will. And even Jesus, who was operating under the authority of His Father during His earthly ministry, still needed people's permission to do a miracle in their lives.

> **John 5:19 (NKJV)**
> *Then Jesus answered and said to them, "Most assuredly, I say to you, the Son can do nothing of Himself, but what He sees the Father do; for whatever He does, the Son also does in like manner."*

For instance, in the New Testament, we see that every person who came to Christ was healed when they asked Him for healing, because they came of their own free will. They submitted to Him, acknowledging that He had spiritual authority, and said, "Lord, I need something from You." As a result of their submission and faith, Jesus healed them.

We don't see a lot of instances where Jesus walked up to someone to initiate ministry. And if He did, He always asked, "Do you want to be healed?" He had to get the person's permission to work in their life. In fact, He couldn't do many miracles in Nazareth because of their unbelief. In other words, they didn't accept His authority to work in their lives, so He didn't.

It's true that we have been given authority in the Earth to represent Jesus, but what if someone doesn't want our help? If we ask someone, "Would you like me to pray for you?" and they say, "No," there's nothing we can do to help them except pray that God will open their eyes to His truth.

Whenever the Gospel is preached, the ultimate goal is to set people free and heal them. However, if they're not willing to listen and receive the Word of God with reverence, then there's not much we can do for them. We can't enforce God's will on them. This is why it's important to remember that our authority over the devil does not mean we have authority over people—unless those people belong to our realm of authority.

What Happens When a Dangerous Situation Arises?

What do we do when a dangerous, destructive situation arises and invades our realm of authority? In such cases, we can exercise spiritual authority over the situation, praying for God to bring about good.

For example, I live in Oklahoma. There are a lot of tornadoes that come through our State. One time, a tornado was approaching the student housing complex of Rhema Bible Training College. A lumber store and a shopping center were located on the same side of the street as the student housing. Of course, the Bible students immediately began to rebuke the storm in the Name of Jesus.

Miraculously, the tornado lifted up and safely passed over student housing, leaving the housing and the students untouched. Both the lumber store and shopping center were destroyed. This is an example of how we as believers can exercise our authority over situations that affect our realm of authority—such as the places where we live and work.

Now, sometimes we can stand in the place of an intercessor and pray the protection of God over other people who don't know Him. We can exercise our spiritual authority in that way, believing God for good things in their lives. And when people come to us requesting our help, we can exercise spiritual authority in that situation. In essence, when somebody asks us to pray for them, they are submitting themselves to us regarding the issue they are seeking prayer for. They're saying, "I'm putting myself in your hands. I believe in your authority to do something about my problem."

And that gives us the right to pray for them and expect results. This is possible because we have authority over our realm—the areas of family, ministry, and work—and all the things God has given us. We have been given authority, in Jesus, to bless others.

Acts 5:29 (NKJV)
But Peter and the other apostles answered and said: "We ought to obey God rather than men."

In Acts chapter 5, the religious leaders of the synagogue tried to prevent the believers, including Peter, from preaching the Gospel. Peter answered them by saying, "I'm sorry, but we must obey God rather than men." Why? Because the higher authority, Jesus, had declared, "Go preach this Gospel." The mandate Jesus gave Christians in the Great Commission overrides any human authority—even if that authority passes laws that say the Gospel cannot be preached.

Authority Starts with Submission to Something

To properly, fully walk in the authority we have in Jesus, we must recognize who and what we must submit to, as well as what we can exercise our authority over. This understanding will greatly enhance our successes in exercising authority. First, we are under God. He is the primary authority that supersedes all others.

But remember: It is God who instituted natural authorities as well. If someone is a criminal, they are violating the authority God put in place. Exercising spiritual authority is next to impossible if one is breaking the law. Likewise, it will be hard to exercise spiritual authority if we are causing trouble within our local church and refusing to submit to our pastor.

I've seen many Christians cause problems for their pastors and cause divisions in the church. Such people inevitably open themselves up for Satan to come in and destroy their lives. Because of this, I oftentimes counsel people that they have two choices when they have complaints about where they work: Either God told you to work there, or He didn't. If God told you to work there, then He knows what it's like to work there, and He expects you to submit to the authorities there.

The only option, if God really told you to be where you are right now, is to represent Him honorably and help change things for good. On the other hand, if God didn't tell you to be where you are right now, then it is time to find out where He wants you, and go there. This way, you'll be in His will and can be a blessing where He has planted you.

Authority to Share the Gospel

Another area where Christians always have authority is in sharing the Gospel. Jesus said, "All authority in Heaven and Earth is Mine. Go and preach." There are no laws of man that have greater authority than Jesus' commands. Through the preaching of the Gospel, God has given us a way to help change those we don't have authority over.

CHAPTER 12

AUTHORITY IN PRAYER

The number one area for believers to exercise our dominion and authority in Jesus' Name is in the realm of prayer. Prayer is an important part of a believer's life. Unfortunately, in much of the Church today, many Christians have no idea how to pray effectively. Praying has become either a ritualistic thing they do, or it becomes a hard thing. A lot of people don't even understand the importance of prayer.

John Wesley, the great Methodist minister who helped bring revival to the United States and England in the 1700s, reportedly said, "It seems to me that without God, we cannot. But without us, He will not." God has chosen to be interdependent with us as His Body in the Earth. He has tied Himself to us, relying on us to use the authority He has given us so that His will is done in the Earth.

And so, God has commissioned us to use prayer, because it's the way in which He works through us to bring about His purposes and plans. As believers, therefore, we are powerful in prayer—because we are in Christ. This is a spiritual reality, yet many Christians don't realize their power in prayer, so they don't use it or tap into it effectively.

To help illustrate the vast strength and mighty power that awaits us in prayer, if we will just believe and act on it, let's look at several examples of how effective prayer works.

The Power of Prayer in Church History

There are so many historical examples of the power of prayer. We'll touch on just a few circumstances here.

First, let's consider a man named John Knox, the founder of the Presbyterian Church. During the period that the Protestant Reformation was happening in Europe, Scotland experienced a revival led by Knox. Many people came to Christ in those days. At the same time, Mary, Queen of the Scots, opposed the Protestants and killed many of them, trying to stamp out the Reformation. In spite of her power, she is recorded as saying, "I fear the prayers of John Knox more than all the assembled armies of Europe."[5]

It says something about a person's prayer life when others say they believe the person has power in prayer, doesn't it? And Knox is not the only historical church figure who had such impact through his prayer life.

Consider Charles Finney, who was one of the greatest revivalists of America's history. Finney ministered in the period right before the American Civil War. He conducted revivals throughout the Northern United States, and whole cities turned to Christ. Bars would shut down because they had no customers. Theaters would close down because nobody would attend plays. Finney carried with him such a strong presence of God that when he would go on a tour of a factory, for example, the owners would have to make sure that all the people stopped working and got off the equipment because in Finney's presence, people would start falling down and crying in conviction for God to save them.[6]

---

5 Knox, J. (1553). Treatise on prayer.

6 Wessel, H. (1810). The autobiography of Charles G. Finney. Bloomington, MI: Bethany House Publishers.

Finney himself was a man of prayer, but he also had a prayer partner known as Father Daniel Nash, who was a man of travail and intercession. Nash would go two weeks ahead of time into a city and begin to pray before Charles Finney ever got there. His prayers penetrated the spiritual atmosphere of the place, so when Finney came in, the glory of God fell. Revival broke out.

Throughout history, there have been people like John Wesley, John Knox, Charles Finney, Daniel Nash, David Brainerd, Rees Howells and others whose names are well-known because they impacted their generation, because they were people of prayer. We tend to think that these instances are rarities or unusual circumstances. But in God's Kingdom, the life-changing power of prayer is the norm, and we can all take part in it as believers.

Lord, Teach Us to Pray

In the book of Luke, there are two chapters that give us specific instructions about prayer. As we look at these passages of Scripture, we're going to see something that I believe can revolutionize the Church's prayer life. Whenever I've taught this concept, it lights a fire in believers and empowers them to engage in a more effective prayer life.

> **Luke 11:1**
> *And it came to pass, that, as He [Jesus] was praying in a certain place, when He ceased, one of His disciples said unto Him, Lord, teach us to pray, as John [the Baptist] also taught his disciples.*

In this passage of Luke, we learn that Jesus was praying, and His disciples were seeing the results of His prayers. By this time in their lives, they had been following Him for a while. They'd seen the dead raised, the blind see, the lame walk, and devils cast out. They'd witnessed all the miracles that Jesus had been performing.

As the disciples were watching and listening to Jesus pray, they could see by the fruits of His ministry that God the Father heard Jesus' prayers. So, when He was done praying and ministering, they asked Him, "Lord, teach us how to do what you're doing, just as John the Baptist taught his disciples how to pray."

Notice that they didn't say, "Lord, teach us how to heal the sick." They didn't say, "Lord, teach us how to preach and teach like You do." They didn't say, "Lord, teach us how to cast out devils."

They said, "Lord, teach us how to pray," because they understood that whatever was going on between Jesus and the Father to bring about such miracles, **prayer was the secret ingredient.** Prayer was the reason Jesus had daily victories and miracles in His life and ministry. They understood that effectual, fervent prayer (as described in James 5:16) was the driving force behind Jesus' success, and they said, "We want to do that too! Teach us how to pray!"

Notice, too, that Jesus responds to His disciples' request by teaching them some important principles of effective prayer. This tells me that prayer can be taught, that there's a right way and a wrong way to pray, and that we can have instructions on how to pray to get results.

Luke 11:2–4

And He said unto them, When ye pray, say, Our Father which art in heaven, Hallowed be Thy name. Thy kingdom come. Thy will be done, as in heaven, so in earth.

Give us day by day our daily bread.

AUTHORITY IN PRAYER

And forgive us our sins; for we also forgive every one that is indebted to us. And lead us not into temptation; but deliver us from evil.

I'm sure you can probably quote these verses. It's something many of us learn at an early age, no matter which church or denomination we belong to. In fact, I was raised learning that prayer as a young boy, and I know it by heart. We call this the Lord's Prayer—and I'll teach you something about this prayer that may just transform your prayer life.

In the original Greek language in which these verses were written, every verb in this prayer is in "the imperative command, present tense." So, really, this is how that prayer should be translated:

Matthew 6:9–13 (ONMB)
Our Father, Who is in the heavens: Your Name must at once be made holy:

Your kingdom must now come: Your will must be done right now, as in Heaven also on Earth:

You must now give us today the things necessary for our existence:

You must right now forgive our sins for us, in the same manner as we have completed forgiving everyone of everything, big and little, against us:

And do not lead us into temptation, but You must now rescue us from the evil one.

That doesn't sound like a passive prayer, does it? That sounds like sticking with it and being determined and bold until you receive the answer you need. One New Testament Greek scholar said the insinuation there in the Greek is as though you're stomping your feet and demanding, "Your will must be done right now! Your Kingdom must come now! You must give us today what we need! You must rescue us right now from the devil!"

This is a prayer based on the authority of the believer. Yet many Christians have not seen this; many of us have missed the point of this set of verses. Jesus wasn't teaching us a rote prayer to repeat. He was teaching us how to pray with authority, demanding that the will of God be done in every situation.

Remember, the world has two kingdoms. We're in the kingdom of God. We've been delivered from the kingdom of darkness. We're not praying that a physical kingdom manifest itself, but we're saying the rule of Heaven must overrule the rule of Satan in our situation. When we say, "God, Your Kingdom come," we are saying that the devil's kingdom has to get out of the way. When we pray this prayer, we're saying, "God, Your will must be done now! Your Kingdom must rule! Your authority must rule in this situation now!"

Be Persistent in Prayer

God's Kingdom is meant to rule in our lives. And we have every right to believe and pray for His will to be done in our lives. But we have to contend for His Kingdom to come, and for His will to be done. It doesn't just fall on us automatically! That's why Jesus followed up His teaching on prayer with the following parable.

> ### Luke 11:5–8
> *And He said unto them, Which of you shall have a friend, and shall go unto him at midnight, and say unto him, Friend, lend me three loaves;*
>
> *For a friend of mine in his journey is come to me, and I have nothing to set before him?*

And he from within shall answer and say, Trouble me not: the door is now shut, and my children are with me in bed; I cannot rise and give thee.

I say unto you, Though he will not rise and give him, because he is his friend, yet because of his importunity he will rise and give him as many as he needeth.

In these verses, Jesus explains that even though we might ignore a friend's request, we won't ignore someone who stays persistent in making their request until we give in to their desire. The lesson for us? Persistence in prayer is essential to receiving an answered prayer.

Smith Wigglesworth once said, "I get more out of believing God for five minutes than by shouting at Him all night long."[7] If we can learn to talk to God honestly and pray in faith the way He tells us to pray, then we can expect to receive more from God than if we groan and moan all night long and shed tears. Yes, there's a place and time for sharing our emotions with God. But emotional displays do not produce results in prayer. And it is not the length of the prayer—but rather our faith in God—that connects us to the answers we desire.

As Jesus shares the parable of a friend seeking bread at midnight, He is sharing more about how to pray and get results. And He goes on to share even more about the importance of being persistent and refusing to quit when we pray.

Luke 11:10–13
For every one that asketh receiveth; and he that seeketh findeth; and to him that knocketh it shall be opened.

---

[7] Frodsham, S. H. (1948). Smith Wigglesworth apostle of faith. Springfield, MO: Gospel Publishing House.

If a son shall ask bread of any of you that is a father, will he give him a stone? or if he ask a fish, will he for a fish give him a serpent?

Or if he shall ask an egg, will he offer him a scorpion?

If ye then, being evil, know how to give good gifts unto your children: how much more shall your heavenly Father give the Holy Spirit to them that ask him?

This set of verses is still related to the story Jesus told of the friend knocking on the door, saying, "I need some food." The words *ask*, *seek*, and *knock* in the original Greek language of the passage indicates that we are to be determined, saying, "I'm not letting go. I'm not giving up." We are to keep on asking, knocking, and seeking until an answer comes.

Then, Jesus goes on to say, "If a son shall ask for bread, his father is not going to give him a stone. If he asks for a fish, the father is not going to give him a serpent. If he asks for an egg, the father will not give him a scorpion. Even human parents, with their frailties and tendencies to sin, want to be generous to their children. They want to give them what they ask for, if they can. If we know how to give good gifts to our children, shouldn't we expect that God the Father knows how to give good things, such as the Holy Spirit, to those who ask Him?"

In other words, we don't have to worry about God's intentions for us. He's not going to give us something that we don't want—something that is dangerous or bad for us—when we pray. God's a good God, and He loves us, and He desires to bless us.

The Power of Importunity

> **Luke 11:8**
> *I say unto you, Though he will not rise and give him, because he is his friend, yet because of his importunity he will rise and give him as many as he needeth.*

An essential key to success in prayer is what the King James Bible calls *importunity*. This word is related to the word *impudence,* which according to the dictionary means being offensively bold, or displaying offensively bold behavior.

Jewish people often refer to this attitude and behavior as *chutzpah*. In English, we might call it *guts*. We might say, "That takes a lot of nerve." This type of importunity, persistence, chutzpah, or guts is such bold behavior, such insistence, that it could be considered offensive. But as we look in the Bible, we see that this attitude gets God's attention.

Consider, as an example, the faithful servant of God, Abraham.

> **Genesis 12:1–3**
> *Now the Lord had said unto Abram, Get thee out of thy country, and from thy kindred, and from thy father's house, unto a land that I will shew thee:*
>
> *And I will make of thee a great nation, and I will bless thee, and make thy name great; and thou shalt be a blessing:*
>
> *And I will bless them that bless thee, and curse him that curseth thee: and in thee shall all families of the earth be blessed.*

God called Abraham and promised him blessings. He directed Abraham to leave his home and go to a foreign land, and He said, "Abraham, I'm going to give you this land. I'm going to give you children."

Abraham did as God commanded. He moved to the land where God led him. He trusted God to see the promised blessings. But many years passed, and Abraham remained childless. So, when God spoke to him again in Genesis 15:1, saying, *Fear not, Abram: I am thy shield, and thy exceeding great reward,* Abraham showed some chutzpah, some importunity.

> **Genesis 15:2–3**
>
> *And Abram said, Lord God, what wilt thou give me, seeing I go childless, and the steward of my house is this Eliezer of Damascus?*
>
> *And Abram said, Behold, to me thou hast given no seed: and, lo, one born in my house is mine heir.*

This passage goes on through verse 20 of Genesis 15, where we learn that as a result of Abraham's importunity, God entered into a covenant with him. As part of that covenant, God promised Abraham the entire land of Canaan as his heritage—a land that would one day be known as Israel.

Notice that Abraham didn't stop with receiving land as an inheritance. He continued boldly, saying, "You promised me children. But I don't have any children." God repeated His promise to Abraham that He would give him children.

Yet—for a time—Abraham continued to remain childless. And years later, in Genesis 17, God again speaks with Abraham and repeats His promises.

Genesis 17:16

I will bless her [Sarah], and give thee a son also of her: yea, I will bless her, and she shall be a mother of nations; kings of people shall be of her.

At this point, Abraham was 99 years old and past the normal age for fathering children. His wife, Sarah, was also old enough to be beyond the normal child-bearing age. So, Abraham laughed at God's word initially, and he said, "Shall he who is old now bear children?"

God wasn't taken aback by Abraham's question and doubt. Instead, He reiterated His promises to Abraham. And Abraham, who had the guts to continue asking for children, also showed guts in his faith by continuing to believe God's promise, even though by the laws of nature, it should have been impossible for him to father a child at his age.

Eventually, Abraham received in the flesh the promised son and heir, Isaac. And even after Isaac was born, God continued to promise Abraham the land and many descendants. God demonstrated that He did not mind Abraham's boldness in asking to receive what God had promised him.

Persistence in the Face of Danger

We can see similar boldness at work in Abraham's grandson, Jacob. Jacob had a certain amount of tenacity, which we can see in his dealings with his brother, Esau. Early in life, Jacob was a conniver and a bit of a deceiver, always working to get his way. He even tricked his father, Isaac, who was aging and blind, to bless him and give him the elder son's blessing, even though this blessing would have rightly belonged to Esau, who was the elder brother.

As a result, Jacob obtained his father's blessing, but he ended up at

IN MY NAME

enmity with Esau for many years. Esau even vowed to kill Jacob after their father died.

Jacob fled to his uncle Laban's house to escape. And for a while, his life seemed to go well at first. But then, Jacob faced a challenging, frustrating situation. He was manipulated by Laban into marrying the man's older daughter, Leah, before he could marry the younger daughter, Rachel. Now, Jacob had labored for seven years to earn Rachel's hand, so when he realized he had been tricked into marrying Leah, he was angry. Yet he could do nothing other than to work for another seven years to marry Rachel, the woman he truly loved.

Eventually, Jacob had to face Esau again. He sent a message in greeting that he thought would be welcomed. But when he got news that Esau was coming to meet him with four hundred men, he became afraid, worried that Esau wanted to kill him for what he had done to him in the past (Genesis 32:6–7). Jacob decided to divide up his people and send his family on ahead while he remained behind, alone at night at his campsite.

Genesis 32:24–25

And Jacob was left alone; and there wrestled a man with him until the breaking of the day.

And when he saw that he prevailed not against him, he touched the hollow of his thigh; and the hollow of Jacob's thigh was out of joint, as he wrestled with him.

As soon as Jacob was alone, an angel of God appeared to him. Jacob wrestled with the angel until the break of day. And as the sun began to come up, the angel had a staff in his hand, and he touched Jacob's hip, and Jacob's hip went out of joint. Have you ever wondered why the angel didn't do that at the beginning? He could have, of course. He had power over Jacob, but he was allowing Jacob to wrestle him.

And what does it mean that Jacob wrestled with this heavenly being? I believe one way to look at this is to consider Jacob's behavior to be like prayer. Sometimes, we feel as though we are wrestling to be heard. And like Jacob, we may be facing such a life-threatening situation that we can't afford to let go of God until we receive the answer we need. Jacob's behavior is a perfect picture of persistence and importunity in prayer.

> **Genesis 32:26–29**
>
> *And he said, Let me go, for the day breaketh. And he said, I will not let thee go, except thou bless me.*
>
> *And he said unto him, What is thy name? And he said, Jacob.*
>
> *And he said, Thy name shall be called no more Jacob, but Israel: for as a prince hast thou power with God and with men, and hast prevailed.*
>
> *And Jacob asked him, and said, Tell me, I pray thee, thy name. And he said, Wherefore is it that thou dost ask after my name? And he blessed him there.*

Jacob declared to the angel, "I will not let you go unless you bless me." Here, we see Jacob's importunity—his persistence in receiving what he desired from God.

As a result of Jacob's persistence, the angel answered and said, "No longer are you going to be called Jacob, but your name will be Prince of God because you have prevailed with God and with man."

When the angel disappeared, Jacob thought, "I just saw God face to face!" He realized that he had been wrestling with God. Yet God allowed Jacob to wrestle with Him. Why did He allow it? I believe God wanted to see how serious Jacob was about receiving what he wanted. Jacob was very serious about it—he persisted, so he prevailed! And as a result, Jacob and Esau were reconciled.

Persistence When Life Gets Desperate

As we go down through history, we see many people have had similar encounters with God. They need something so desperately that they will not give up until they receive what they need—and God meets them at the point of that need to do a miracle!

Do you remember the story of the Shunammite woman who ministered to Elisha in 2 Kings 4? She had no children, so Elisha prayed for her and told her she would have a son, even though her husband was elderly. And it came to pass that she did indeed give birth to a son.

But when the son had become a young man, he suddenly and unexpectedly died. The Shunammite woman was so upset, so devastated and desperate, that she went to seek Elisha. And when she found him, she confronted him.

> **2 Kings 4:28–30**
>
> *Then she said, Did I desire a son of my lord? did I not say, Do not deceive me?*
>
> *Then he said to Gehazi, Gird up thy loins, and take my staff in thine hand, and go thy way: if thou meet any man, salute him not; and if any salute thee, answer him not again: and lay my staff upon the face of the child.*
>
> *And the mother of the child said, As the Lord liveth, and as thy soul liveth, I will not leave thee. And he arose, and followed her.*

The woman essentially demanded that Elisha do something about the death of her son. She even refused to leave him alone until a miracle happened, and her son was brought back from the dead. She received her miracle because she would not quit until she received it.

We see this same determination and importunity in the New Testament with the woman who had an issue of blood. She had suffered her illness for many years, but no one could heal her. And because she was continually bleeding, according to the Jewish law, she was not supposed to leave her home and be in public. It must have been a lonely, depressing twelve years.

Then one day, this woman heard that Jesus was nearby. She was desperate, and she was determined to receive a miracle from Him. So, as soon as she heard He was passing by, she headed out to where He was, pressing right through the crowd to get to Him. All the time she was doing this, she was telling herself, by faith, "If I can just touch His garment, I'm going to be healed."

Mark 5:25–34

And a certain woman, which had an issue of blood twelve years,

And had suffered many things of many physicians, and had spent all that she had, and was nothing bettered, but rather grew worse,

When she had heard of Jesus, came in the press behind, and touched His garment.

For she said, If I may touch but His clothes, I shall be whole.

And straightway the fountain of her blood was dried up; and she felt in her body that she was healed of that plague.

And Jesus, immediately knowing in Himself that virtue had gone out of Him, turned Him about in the press, and said, Who touched My clothes?

And His disciples said unto Him, Thou seest the multitude thronging thee, and sayest thou, Who touched Me?

And He looked round about to see her that had done this thing.

But the woman fearing and trembling, knowing what was done in her, came and fell down before Him, and told Him all the truth.

And He said unto her, Daughter, thy faith hath made thee whole; go in peace, and be whole of thy plague.

Pressing through a throng of people to reach Jesus must have been hard for this woman, but she did it. She didn't quit. As soon as she neared Jesus, she touched him, just as she was determined to do. And at that moment, Jesus felt the power of God flow through Him. He said, "Whoa, somebody touched Me!"

His disciples were all around Him, feeling the press of the enormous crowd against them, and they said, "Are You kidding me? There's all this crowd! Of course, people are touching You!"

"No," Jesus said. "I mean, somebody touched Me in faith."

The woman came trembling before Him to tell Him what she had done, frightened that He might have her punished for being out in public while she was bleeding. But He didn't do anything of the kind. Instead, Jesus told the woman, "Your faith made you whole."

This may shock you. This may challenge your theology. But Jesus didn't have anything to do with this woman's healing, except for being present as a point of contact for her faith. He didn't even know she was present in the crowd. The woman herself initiated her miracle with her determination, telling herself, "I'm going to get what I need today." And she did! She received the healing she was desperate to receive.

Persistence in the Face of Initial Resistance

Sometimes, we find ourselves being persistent in prayer even when it seems everyone is telling us the answer is impossible.

We see this in the experience of Jesus and the Syrophoenician woman. Jesus was traveling in the northern parts of Israel along the coast, when a Syrophoenician woman came to Him and cried out, "My daughter is home oppressed by a demon! Set her free!"

Surprisingly, Jesus seemed to ignore her. He didn't even talk to her at first. The woman ran after Him, while He continued walking. And she continued to beg Him to set her daughter free. Her insistence grew so annoying to the disciples that they said to Jesus, "Would you send her away?"

He didn't send her away. But He did turn to her and say, "It's not right to take the children's bread and give it to the dogs."

Now, the Canaanites were not part of the covenant God had with Israel. They were outsiders, and many Jewish people in that day were not kind to them. Jesus was not being critical of the woman, but He was willing to test her faith and her persistence. So He said something to her that might have put her off if she wasn't determined to receive a miracle from God.

But the Syrophoenician woman didn't waver in her determination. She came closer, fell at Jesus' feet, and said, "Yes, but even the dogs get the crumbs that fall from the table."

Talk about persistence! Talk about importunity! What a bold statement she made that day. She was willing to take anything that God offered her, because she was desperate and determined to see her daughter restored, no matter what. And the result of her importunity? Victory!

Jesus said, "Woman, great is your faith. You have what you want." And her daughter, the Scriptures tell us, was healed from that moment on.

Can you see a common denominator here? There is no such thing as wimpy, passive faith. Faith is not passive. Faith is determined, and faith has chutzpah. Faith has guts. It refuses to quit until it receives an answer.

Prayer Is Based on Our Legal Rights in Heaven

Luke 18:1–8

And he spake a parable unto them to this end, that men ought always to pray, and not to faint;

Saying, There was in a city a judge, which feared not God, neither regarded man:

And there was a widow in that city; and she came unto him, saying, Avenge me of mine adversary.

And he would not for a while: but afterward he said within himself, Though I fear not God, nor regard man;

Yet because this widow troubleth me, I will avenge her, lest by her continual coming she weary me.

And the Lord said, Hear what the unjust judge saith.

And shall not God avenge his own elect, which cry day and night unto him, though he bear long with them?

I tell you that he will avenge them speedily. Nevertheless when the Son of man cometh, shall he find faith on the earth?

Jesus declared that the purpose of this parable was to teach us *that men ought always to pray, and not to faint.* This tells me that there will come times in prayer that we will be tempted to faint, to get exhausted, to give up. But this parable is to be an example to us of why we should refuse to quit.

The whole setting of this story is a courtroom in which we see a judge, a person in need, and an adversary. That word *adversary* appears in 1 Peter 5:8, which says, "The devil, your adversary, as a roaring lion roams to and fro, seeking whom he may devour." *Adversary* literally means "against your rights," or, "one who brings a lawsuit against you." The devil is the adversary, or the one who brings a lawsuit against us in the courts of Heaven to try to say we have no rights.

The accuser of the brethren accuses us before God day and night. And what he uses against us is words—words of condemnation, words of accusation, words of blame. The devil believes in the power of words. That's why he's the accuser. He's using words against us.

He's trying to convince us that we don't have the rights we have, because as soon as he gets us to believe we don't have rights to healing, deliverance, freedom, and God's blessings, he can control us. And if he can keep us from receiving what God has for us, he can hinder us from putting him in his place, under our feet.

But of course, as believers, we do have rights in the courts of Heaven. God has declared us righteous in Christ. To be righteous means we are people who have rights, because God has declared us free of accusations and forgiven us of any debts we owed Him through sin. And He has invested in us the same rights that Jesus, His Son, has. That's what it means to be co-heirs with Christ (Romans 8:17).

Remember, Adam and Eve were slaves to sin. They had no rights. But Jesus made us righteous through His resurrection. In other words, He restored rights to us. Our righteousness is not based upon what we do, but on our faith in Him and what He's done for us. He grants us righteousness by His will; we don't earn it. So, the rights He has given to us have nothing to do with our accomplishments, but rather, they are based in simply believing in what He has done.

This righteousness we receive through faith in Christ gives us authority over the devil. And it gives us a right to pray in faith, expecting answers from God. We have every right to pray and believe God for His will to be done.

God has given us His Word, and He wants us to use His Word against our adversary when we pray.

> **Revelation 12:11**
> *And they overcame him by the blood of the Lamb, and by the word of their testimony; and they loved not their lives unto the death.*

The blood of the Lamb defeats the devil in our lives because that shed blood is what gives us our rights. Though the devil accuses us day and night, the blood of Jesus never ceases to speak on our behalf. Jesus is always making intercession for us before God's throne. And the Holy Ghost intercedes for us too. And the word of our testimony matters also, because we are in God's courtroom. We can use God's Word in prayer and overcome the accusations of the devil.

> **Romans 8:31–39**
>
> *What shall we then say to these things? If God be for us, who can be against us?*
>
> *He that spared not his own Son, but delivered him up for us all, how shall he not with him also freely give us all things?*
>
> *Who shall lay any thing to the charge of God's elect? It is God that justifieth.*
>
> *Who is he that condemneth? It is Christ that died, yea rather, that is risen again, who is even at the right hand of God, who also maketh intercession for us.*
>
> *Who shall separate us from the love of Christ? shall tribulation, or distress, or persecution, or famine, or nakedness, or peril, or sword?*
>
> *As it is written, For thy sake we are killed all the day long; we are accounted as sheep for the slaughter.*
>
> *Nay, in all these things we are more than conquerors through him that loved us.*
>
> *For I am persuaded, that neither death, nor life, nor angels, nor principalities, nor powers, nor things present, nor things to come,*
>
> *Nor height, nor depth, nor any other creature, shall be able to separate us from the love of God, which is in Christ Jesus our Lord.*

Keep this powerful truth in mind—the court of God is rigged in our favor as believers, because the Judge is our Father, our number one Attorney (or Advocate) is His Son, Jesus, and our number two Attorney is the Holy Ghost. The witness is the "blood that speaks better things." Who is going to bring a charge against us, and who is going to condemn you? Not the Father, not the Son, not the Holy Spirit!

> **1 John 2:1**
> *My little children, these things write I unto you, that ye sin not. And if any man sin, we have an advocate with the Father, Jesus Christ the righteous.*

The word *advocate* here is from the Greek word *parakletos*. It means "one who pleads another's cause before a judge for defense as a legal assistant." Whenever the devil shows up and tries to steal our rights, we have an Advocate—Jesus Himself—pleading our case before God.

> **1 John 3:20–22**
> *For if our heart condemn us, God is greater than our heart, and knoweth all things.*
>
> *Beloved, if our heart condemn us not, then have we confidence toward God.*
>
> *And whatsoever we ask, we receive of him, because we keep his commandments, and do those things that are pleasing in his sight.*

What the enemy tries to do is make us feel so much guilt and shame that we cannot stand and defend our rights in Heaven's courts. By robbing us of confidence and faith, he makes it hard for us to believe God. As 1 John says, if our heart condemns us, we don't have confidence with God. But if our heart doesn't condemn us, then we have confidence with God. And it is easier for us to receive all we ask for in prayer when we are in faith about it, and confident that He hears us.

Base Your Prayers on the Evidence—God's Word

In the Bible, the terms used to refer to prayer—intercession, petition, and supplication—are all legal terms. When we understand that prayer is a form of legal entreaty, based in God's laws and our righteous status in Him, we can come into prayer with a greater understanding of our authority. Our prayers are meant to be based on the evidence supplied in God's Word that we have the right to what we are asking for.

Our prayers are not based on our efforts, or our work. They're not based on our feelings either. Our prayers are to be based on the Word of God. We come with a legal document—His Word, the Bible—into the courts of Heaven to obtain what we need.

Is the devil trying to steal your children? You have a legal document that says, "believe on the Lord Jesus Christ, and you and your whole house shall be saved" (Acts 16:31). You have a legal document that talks about binding the enemy, casting out devils, and loosing things (Matthew 16:19). You have a legal document that declares the seed of the righteous shall be delivered (Proverbs 11:21). And there are many other scriptural pieces of evidence you can search out and use as you create your petition to go before the Judge in prayer.

I wouldn't want to be the devil in a case tried in the courts of God against a believer. Why? Because he has lost the case before it even starts! On our side, we have God the Father, Jesus the Son, and the Holy Spirit all in collaboration together. The Judge and the Attorneys are at work on our behalf. And because of what Christ has done for us through the Cross, the evidence in our favor is already laid out. The documentation for the petitions we are making has already been accepted by the court. The devil can't win—unless we allow him to win.

The problem is, most Christians don't realize the full extent of their victory over the devil. They'll get in the courtroom and agree with their enemy. But remember, Jesus defeated the devil, stripped him of his legal rights and his armaments, and overpowered him in the Resurrection! The only thing the devil has going in his favor is if he can get us to testify against ourselves, because then he can build a case against us.

We should not be agreeing with the devil on anything. Instead, we are to use the word of our testimony wisely, in agreement with God and His Word. So, when we testify, what do we say? We go to the evidence. We go to God's Word, and we say what His Word says. We agree with God. We testify only to what the Bible says is true—in Christ, we are healed, forgiven, delivered, free and victorious over all the works of the enemy. We testify according to the evidence in God's Word. This shuts down the adversary, and he will end up fleeing from us.

So, what are you praying about right now? Healing? Your family? Your job? Your finances? You have a right to enter God's courts with praise and thanksgiving. You have a right to stand in faith on His Word, talk to the Judge, and plead your case alongside your Attorneys, knowing that they're pleading your case too. And you can stand on the blood of Jesus, rebuke the adversary, and tell him, "You're a liar! I rebuke you in the Name of Jesus!" Stand in faith for your family, your health, and your finances. You have the right!

You Have the Right to Pray for Others as Well as Yourself

As a believer, you have every right to pray not only for your own personal needs and situations, but also to go before God in faith, believing and praying on behalf of others. This is called intercession—which simply means going into court and pleading with the Judge on behalf of somebody who either can't go, doesn't know how to go, or refuses to do it on their own. Intercession is something every believer can do on behalf of those they care about and interact with—such as family, friends, and coworkers who need the Lord in their lives.

AUTHORITY IN PRAYER

This technique works because of another type of legal precedent known as "the power of attorney." When you give someone the power of attorney, it gives them the authority to execute certain legal actions on your behalf, such as signing a contract or a document. When someone has the power of attorney for you, they can sign your name, and it will be as though you signed the document personally.

When Jesus ascended to Heaven after the Resurrection, He gave us—His Body, His Church—the power of attorney. He gave us His Name! He said, "Up to now, you haven't asked anything in My Name, but ask and it shall be given to you" (John 16:24). He said, "In My Name, you will cast out devils, lay hands on the sick, and speak with new tongues" (Mark 16:17–18). We've been called by His Name, baptized in His Name, filled with the Holy Ghost in His Name, sent out in His Name, and commissioned to use His Name.

So, when we come across a demon or a sick person, we just take out that power of attorney, and we speak to the issue in the Name of Jesus. When we do so, it's as though Jesus Himself is standing there saying to that demon, "Get out!" It's as though Jesus Himself is saying to that sick person, "Be healed! Rise and walk!"

When you know someone who is suffering from sickness, pray for them in faith, demanding God's will be done. You might pray something like this: "God, by the stripes of Jesus, my friend was healed. Your wounds healed him. You paid the price. This is the will of God. Your will must be done now! Your kingdom must rule now. You must overcome this darkness, this satanic attack. It's not Your will. We're contending for Your will, God."

Now, if you are praying for unbelievers, they're still under the dominion of the devil. So, you'll have to continue standing in intercession for them. It's a repeated act. You regularly go to God on their behalf, praying for their salvation and deliverance until results come.

How you intercede for others to receive salvation, using the Name of Jesus, is simple. You go before God, mention the person's name, and plead the blood of Jesus over them. For example, you could say, "Father, the blood of Jesus was shed for the sins of the whole world, and so I'm pleading the blood for this person. I forgive them, in Jesus' Name, based on the blood of Jesus. I extend Your forgiveness and mercy to them."

Do you know what you've just done when you've prayed like that for someone? You've given the Holy Ghost access into their life. He can begin to convict them and draw them to God.

Prayer Is Partnership with God

This life is training for reigning. We are to learn now, in this life, how to live and reign in partnership with God, as joint-heirs with Christ. And prayer is the number one place where we train to reign. It is the number one way we exercise spiritual authority because through the prayer realm, nations change, kingdoms rise and fall, people are saved, healed, and delivered, ministries are birthed, jobs are formed, and inventions are created. It happens first in the realm of prayer, and then it comes into being in the natural realm.

You can change your situation. You can change the place where you live. You can change the atmosphere in a place. You can influence your family, community, and even your nation when you realize who you are and what you have in Christ.

I challenge you in the name of Jesus to pray every day in faith, with persistence and importunity. Throw away your religious prayers. Throw out every unscriptural, wimpy, powerless, impotent prayer that you've ever prayed, and begin to pray with the boldness and determination that Jesus taught us to use in prayer. Take your place before God in authority. Believe and pursue in faith what Jesus declared to His disciples: "I'm going to build my Church, and the gates of hell will not stop it."

Know this. When you open your mouth in prayer, you are taking your place before God, the Creator of the universe, and joining with Him in faith—because He's forever bound Himself to work through us. His will on Earth has to be done through us.

CHAPTER 13

OVERCOMING SCRIPTURES

The following verses are suggestions for you to use as you continue to build your faith on this topic. Look them up in your Bible, meditate on them, memorize them, and add some more to this list. I trust these will help you get started on a continual learning process.

Genesis 1:27–30

So God created man in His own image, in the image of God created He him; male and female created He them.

And God blessed them, and God said unto them, Be fruitful, and multiply, and replenish the Earth, and subdue it: and have dominion over the fish of the sea, and over the fowl of the air, and over every living thing that moveth upon the earth.

And God said, Behold, I have given you every herb bearing seed, which is upon the face of all the Earth, and every tree, in the which is the fruit of a tree yielding seed; to you it shall be for meat.

And to every beast of the earth, and to every fowl of the air, and to every thing that creepeth upon the Earth, wherein there is life, I have given every green herb for meat: and it was so.

Isaiah 54:17

No weapon that is formed against thee shall prosper; and every tongue that shall rise against thee in judgment thou shalt condemn. This is the heritage of the servants of the Lord, and their righteousness is of Me, saith the Lord.

Matthew 10:1, 7–8

And when He had called unto Him His twelve disciples, He gave them power against unclean spirits, to cast them out, and to heal all manner of sickness and all manner of disease.

And as ye go, preach, saying, The Kingdom of Heaven is at hand.

Heal the sick, cleanse the lepers, raise the dead, cast out devils: freely ye have received, freely give.

Matthew 16:18–19 (NKJV)

And I also say to you that you are Peter, and on this rock I will build My Church, and the gates of Hades shall not prevail against it.

And I will give you the keys of the Kingdom of Heaven, and whatever you bind on Earth will be bound in Heaven, and whatever you loose on Earth will be loosed in Heaven.

Matthew 28:18–20 (NKJV)

And Jesus came and spoke to them, saying, "All authority has been given to Me in Heaven and on Earth.

Go therefore and make disciples of all the nations, baptizing them in the Name of the Father and of the Son and of the Holy Spirit,

Teaching them to observe all things that I have commanded you; and lo, I am with you always, even to the end of the age."

Mark 16:15–20 (NKJV)

And He said to them, "Go into all the world and preach the Gospel to every creature.

He who believes and is baptized will be saved; but he who does not believe will be condemned.

And these signs will follow those who believe: In My name they will cast out demons; they will speak with new tongues;

They will take up serpents; and if they drink anything deadly, it will by no means hurt them; they will lay hands on the sick, and they will recover."

So then, after the Lord had spoken to them, He was received up into Heaven, and sat down at the right hand of God.

And they went out and preached everywhere, the Lord working with them and confirming the Word through the accompanying signs.

Luke 4:16–21 (NKJV)

So He came to Nazareth, where He had been brought up. And as His custom was, He went into the synagogue on the Sabbath day, and stood up to read.

And He was handed the book of the prophet Isaiah. And when He had opened the book, He found the place where it was written:

"The Spirit of the Lord is upon Me, because He has anointed Me to preach the Gospel to the poor; He has sent Me to heal the brokenhearted, to proclaim liberty to the captives and recovery of sight to the blind, to set at liberty those who are oppressed;

To proclaim the acceptable year of the Lord."

Then He closed the book, and gave it back to the attendant and sat down. And the eyes of all who were in the synagogue were fixed on Him.

And He began to say to them, "Today this Scripture is fulfilled in your hearing."

Luke 10:1, 17–20

After these things the Lord appointed other seventy also, and sent them two and two before His face into every city and place, whither He Himself would come.

And the seventy returned again with joy, saying, Lord, even the devils are subject unto us through Thy Name.

And He said unto them, I beheld Satan as lightning fall from Heaven.

Behold, I give unto you power to tread on serpents and scorpions, and over all the power of the enemy: and nothing shall by any means hurt you.

Notwithstanding in this rejoice not, that the spirits are subject unto you; but rather rejoice, because your names are written in Heaven.

Luke 17:21b

Behold, the Kingdom of God is within you.

John 8:31b–32 (NKJV)

If you abide in My Word, you are My disciples indeed.

And you shall know the truth, and the truth shall make you free.

John 14:12–14

Verily, verily, I say unto you, He that believeth on me, the works that I do shall he do also; and greater works than these shall he do; because I go unto My Father.

And whatsoever ye shall ask in My Name, that will I do, that the Father may be glorified in the Son.

If ye shall ask any thing in My Name, I will do it.

John 16:23–24

And in that day ye shall ask Me nothing. Verily, verily, I say unto you, Whatsoever ye shall ask the Father in My Name, He will give it you.

Hitherto have ye asked nothing in My Name: ask, and ye shall receive, that your joy may be full.

Acts 3:6 (NIV)

Then Peter said, "Silver or gold I do not have, but what I do have I give you. In the Name of Jesus Christ of Nazareth, walk."

Acts 3:16 (NIV)

By faith in the Name of Jesus, this man whom you see and know was made strong. It is Jesus' Name and the faith that comes through Him that has completely healed Him, as you can all see.

Acts 10:38

How God anointed Jesus of Nazareth with the Holy Ghost and with power: who went about doing good, and healing all that were oppressed of the devil; for God was with Him.

Acts 16:16–18

And it came to pass, as we went to prayer, a certain damsel possessed with a spirit of divination met us, which brought her masters much gain by soothsaying:

The same followed Paul and us, and cried, saying, These men are the servants of the most high God, which shew unto us the way of salvation.

And this did she many days. But Paul, being grieved, turned and said to the spirit, I command thee in the name of Jesus Christ to come out of her. And he came out the same hour.

Romans 5:1–2

Therefore being justified by faith, we have peace with God through our Lord Jesus Christ:

By whom also we have access by faith into this grace wherein we stand, and rejoice in hope of the glory of God.

Romans 5:8–9

But God commendeth His love toward us, in that, while we were yet sinners, Christ died for us.

Much more then, being now justified by His blood, we shall be saved from wrath through Him.

Romans 5:17

For if by one man's offence death reigned by one; much more they which receive abundance of grace and of the gift of righteousness shall reign in life by one, Jesus Christ.

Romans 8:1 (NKJV)

There is therefore now no condemnation to those who are in Christ Jesus, who do not walk according to the flesh, but according to the Spirit.

Romans 8:28–29

And we know that all things work together for good to them that love God, to them who are the called according to His purpose.

For whom He did foreknow, He also did predestinate to be conformed to the image of his Son, that He might be the firstborn among many brethren.

Romans 8:37 (NIV)

No, in all these things we are more than conquerors through Him who loved us.

2 Corinthians 5:17

Therefore if any man be in Christ, he is a new creature: old things are passed away; behold, all things are become new.

2 Corinthians 5:21

For He hath made Him to be sin for us, who knew no sin; that we might be made the righteousness of God in Him.

Galatians 2:20

I am crucified with Christ: nevertheless I live; yet not I, but Christ liveth in me: and the life which I now live in the flesh I live by the faith of the Son of God, who loved me, and gave Himself for me.

Galatians 3:13–14

Christ hath redeemed us from the curse of the law, being made a curse for us: for it is written, Cursed is every one that hangeth on a tree:

That the blessing of Abraham might come on the Gentiles through Jesus Christ; that we might receive the promise of the Spirit through faith.

Galatians 3:27–29

For as many of you as have been baptized into Christ have put on Christ.

There is neither Jew nor Greek, there is neither bond nor free, there is neither male nor female: for ye are all one in Christ Jesus.

And if ye be Christ's, then are ye Abraham's seed, and heirs according to the promise.

Ephesians 1:15–2:9

Wherefore I also, after I heard of your faith in the Lord Jesus, and love unto all the saints,

Cease not to give thanks for you, making mention of you in my prayers;

That the God of our Lord Jesus Christ, the Father of glory, may give unto you the spirit of wisdom and revelation in the knowledge of Him:

The eyes of your understanding being enlightened; that ye may know what is the hope of His calling, and what the riches of the glory of his inheritance in the saints,

And what is the exceeding greatness of His power to us-ward who believe, according to the working of His mighty power,

Which He wrought in Christ, when He raised Him from the dead, and set Him at His own right hand in the heavenly places,

OVERCOMING SCRIPTURES

Far above all principality, and power, and might, and dominion, and every name that is named, not only in this world, but also in that which is to come:

And hath put all things under His feet, and gave Him to be the head over all things to the Church,

Which is His Body, the fulness of Him that filleth all in all.

And you hath He quickened, who were dead in trespasses and sins;

Wherein in time past ye walked according to the course of this world, according to the prince of the power of the air, the spirit that now worketh in the children of disobedience:

Among whom also we all had our conversation in times past in the lusts of our flesh, fulfilling the desires of the flesh and of the mind; and were by nature the children of wrath, even as others.

But God, who is rich in mercy, for His great love wherewith He loved us,

Even when we were dead in sins, hath quickened us together with Christ, (by grace ye are saved;)

And hath raised us up together, and made us sit together in heavenly places in Christ Jesus:

That in the ages to come He might shew the exceeding riches of His grace in His kindness toward us through Christ Jesus.

For by grace are ye saved through faith; and that not of yourselves: it is the gift of God:

Not of works, lest any man should boast.

Ephesians 3:1–11
For this cause I Paul, the prisoner of Jesus Christ for you Gentiles,

If ye have heard of the dispensation of the grace of God which is given me to you-ward:

How that by revelation He made known unto me the mystery; (as I wrote afore in few words,

Whereby, when ye read, ye may understand my knowledge in the mystery of Christ)

Which in other ages was not made known unto the sons of men, as it is now revealed unto His holy apostles and prophets by the Spirit;

That the Gentiles should be fellow heirs, and of the same Body, and partakers of his promise in Christ by the Gospel:

Whereof I was made a minister, according to the gift of the grace of God given unto me by the effectual working of His power.

Unto me, who am less than the least of all saints, is this grace given, that I should preach among the Gentiles the unsearchable riches of Christ;

And to make all men see what is the fellowship of the mystery, which from the beginning of the world hath been hid in God, who created all things by Jesus Christ:

To the intent that now unto the principalities and powers in heavenly places might be known by the Church the manifold wisdom of God,

According to the eternal purpose which He purposed in Christ Jesus our Lord.

Ephesians 6:10–18 (NIV)

Finally, be strong in the Lord and in His mighty power.

Put on the full armor of God, so that you can take your stand against the devil's schemes.

For our struggle is not against flesh and blood, but against the rulers, against the authorities, against the powers of this dark world and against the spiritual forces of evil in the heavenly realms.

Therefore put on the full armor of God, so that when the day of evil comes, you may be able to stand your ground, and after you have done everything, to stand.

Stand firm then, with the belt of truth buckled around your waist, with the breastplate of righteousness in place,

And with your feet fitted with the readiness that comes from the Gospel of peace.

In addition to all this, take up the shield of faith, with which you can extinguish all the flaming arrows of the evil one.

Take the helmet of salvation and the sword of the Spirit, which is the Word of God.

And pray in the Spirit on all occasions with all kinds of prayers and requests. With this in mind, be alert and always keep on praying for all the Lord's people.

Philippians 2:5–11

Let this mind be in you, which was also in Christ Jesus:

Who, being in the form of God, thought it not robbery to be equal with God:

But made Himself of no reputation, and took upon Him the form of a servant, and was made in the likeness of men:

And being found in fashion as a man, He humbled Himself, and became obedient unto death, even the death of the Cross.

Wherefore God also hath highly exalted him, and given Him a Name which is above every name:

That at the name of Jesus every knee should bow, of things in Heaven, and things in Earth, and things under the earth;

And that every tongue should confess that Jesus Christ is Lord, to the glory of God the Father.

Colossians 1:12—15

Giving thanks unto the Father, which hath made us meet to be partakers of the inheritance of the saints in light:

Who hath delivered us from the power of darkness, and hath translated us into the Kingdom of his dear Son.

In whom we have redemption through his blood, even the forgiveness of sins:

Who is the image of the invisible God, the firstborn of every creature.

Colossians 1:25—27

Whereof I am made a minister, according to the dispensation of God which is given to me for you, to fulfil the Word of God;

Even the mystery which hath been hid from ages and from generations, but now is made manifest to His saints:

To whom God would make known what is the riches of the glory of this mystery among the Gentiles; which is Christ in you, the hope of glory.

Colossians 2:13—15

And you, being dead in your sins and the uncircumcision of your flesh, hath he quickened together with Him, having forgiven you all trespasses;

Blotting out the handwriting of ordinances that was against us, which was contrary to us, and took it out of the way, nailing it to His Cross;

And having spoiled principalities and powers, He made a shew of them openly, triumphing over them in it.

Hebrews 1:4–5 (NIV)

So He became as much superior to the angels as the Name He has inherited is superior to theirs.

For to which of the angels did God ever say, "You are My Son; today I have become Your Father"? Or again, "I will be His Father, and He will be my Son"?

Hebrews 4:12 (NIV)

For the Word of God is alive and active. Sharper than any double-edged sword, it penetrates even to dividing soul and spirit, joints and marrow; it judges the thoughts and attitudes of the heart.

James 4:7

Submit yourselves therefore to God. Resist the devil, and he will flee from you.

1 Peter 5:8–9 (NKJV)

Be sober, be vigilant; because your adversary the devil walks about like a roaring lion, seeking whom he may devour.

Resist him, steadfast in the faith, knowing that the same sufferings are experienced by your brotherhood in the world.

1 John 3:8

For this purpose the Son of God was manifested, that He might destroy the works of the devil.

1 John 4:4

Greater is He that is in you, than he that is in the world.

Salvation Prayer

Romans 10:9-10 says, "That if thou shalt confess with thy mouth the Lord Jesus, and shalt believe in thine heart that God hath raised him from the dead, thou shalt be saved. For with the heart man believeth unto righteousness; and with the mouth confession is made unto salvation."

If you have never believed and confessed Jesus as your Lord as described in Romans 10:9-10, then you can say the following prayer from your heart:

> *Dear Heavenly Father, I come to You in the Name of Jesus. The Bible says if I confess with my mouth that "Jesus is Lord," and believe in my heart that God raised Him from the dead, I will be saved (Rom. 10:9). I believe with my heart that Jesus is the Son of God and He has risen from the dead, and I confess with my mouth that Jesus is the Lord and Savior of my life. Thank You for saving me!*
>
> *In Jesus' Name I pray. Amen.*